GREAT AUTHORS OF

MYSTERY, HORROR
& THRILLERS

Essential Authors for Children & Teens

GREAT AUTHORS OF

MYSTERY, HORROR & THRILLERS

EDITED BY JEANNE NAGLE

Britannica®
Educational Publishing
IN ASSOCIATION WITH
ROSEN
EDUCATIONAL SERVICES

Published in 2014 by Britannica Educational Publishing (a trademark of Encyclopædia Britannica, Inc.) in association with The Rosen Publishing Group, Inc.
29 East 21st Street, New York, NY 10010

Distributed exclusively by Rosen Publishing.
To see additional Britannica Educational Publishing titles, go to www.rosenpublishing.com

First Edition

Britannica Educational Publishing
J.E. Luebering: Director, Core Reference Group
Anthony L. Green: Editor, Compton's by Britannica

Rosen Publishing
Hope Lourie Killcoyne: Executive Editor
Jeanne Nagle: Senior Editor
Nelson Sá: Art Director
Brian Garvey: Designer
Cindy Reiman: Photography Manager
Introduction by Laura Loria

Cataloging-in-Publication Data

Great authors of mystery, horror & thrillers/[editor] Jeanne Nagle.—First Edition.
    pages cm.—(Essential Authors for Children & Teens)
Includes bibliographical references and index.
ISBN 978-1-62275-094-8 (library binding)
1. Novelists—Biography—Juvenile literature. 2. Detective and mystery stories—History and criticism—Juvenile literature. 3. Horror tales—History and criticism—Juvenile literature. 4. Suspense fiction—History and criticism—Juvenile literature. I. Nagle, Jeanne, editor of compilation.
PN452.G696 2014
809—dc23
[B]

2013026992

Manufactured in the United States of America

Contents

39

58

65

80

86

126

153

164

Crime and bloodshed are often at the heart of mysteries, horror stories, and thrillers. Getty Images

Introduction

There are many readers who enjoy following leads, being scared out of their wits, or otherwise getting their adrenaline coursing through their veins. *Great Authors of Mystery, Horror & Thrillers* is their guide to the writers who specialize in these gripping tales.

Classic mystery novels revolve around attempts to piece together who committed a crime and why. The first recognized mystery tale was "Murders in the Rue Morgue," written by Edgar Allen Poe in 1841. Other early authors of the genre include Sir Arthur Conan Doyle, the creator of Sherlock Holmes.

Mystery novels came of age in stages, growing and adapting as the decades passed. In the 1920s, the "Golden Age" of mysteries, the world was introduced to Agatha Christie's Belgian detective Hercule Poirot and Dorothy L. Sayers's Lord Peter Wimsey. During the first half of the 20th century, "pulp" novels had their heyday, with stories by Dashiell Hammett and Raymond Chandler featuring tough-guy gumshoes in gritty settings. Modern mystery writers, such as Sue Grafton and Dick Francis, continued spinning tales of motive-seeking and clue-hunting.

Young adult mysteries also have been popular. Novels in the *Nancy Drew* and *Hardy Boys* series, created by Edward Stratemeyer but written through the years by a series of authors under the pen name Carolyn Keene, have sold for decades since their publication began in 1930s.

The supernatural, evil, fantastical, and futuristic all find their place in horror novels, new and old. Many classic novels in this genre, including Mary Shelley's *Frankenstein, or The Modern Prometheus*, and Bram Stoker's *Dracula*, enthrall readers to this day. These tales are the subject of many modern and contemporary adaptations, despite being written in the nineteenth century

Modern horror novels are said to have had their birth in the 1970s, beginning in 1974 with the publication of Stephen King's *Carrie*. Peter Straub, Clive Barker, and Anne Rice are among the authors whose novels are popular enough that, as with many of King's works, they have been adapted for the silver screen. Today's young horror readers are particularly taken with the works of Stephenie Meyers, whose *Twilight* series sold 100 million copies and spent 143 weeks on the *New York Times* best-seller's list. The books also spawned a blockbuster film franchise.

Thrillers captivate their readers with suspense. These are plot-driven novels in which character development is rivaled, or even surpassed, by action. Thrillers can be placed in a variety of subcategories. There are spy thrillers, mastered by authors such as John Le Carré and Tom Clancy. Michael Crichton (*The Andromeda Strain*) made a name for himself penning medical thrillers, while legal thrillers were brought to the top of best-seller lists by the likes of John Grisham and Scott Turrow.

All the authors profiled here are considered essential because of their contributions to the types of stories that make people squirm and their hearts race. Through the pages of this book, readers are invited to delve deeper into the lives and craft of their favorite authors in these genres, or become acquainted with writers who may quickly become new favorites.

JOAN AIKEN

(b. 1924–d. 2004)

B ritish author Joan Aiken wrote fantasy, adventure, horror, and suspense stories for both juvenile and adult readers. She is perhaps best known as the inventor of a genre called the "unhistorical romance," which combines humor and action with traditional mythic and fairy-tale elements. Many of these works are set in an invented historical era during the imagined reign of James III (James Edward, the Old Pretender) of England.

Joan Delano Aiken was born on September 4, 1924, in Rye, Sussex, England, the daughter of the poet Conrad Aiken. While still a student, she had two poems published in the prestigious magazine the *Abinger Chronicle*, and when she was 18 years old her first short story was published. As an adult, she wrote radio scripts and worked as a librarian for the United Nations. In 1955 she became an editor for the literary magazine *Argosy* and later was a copywriter for an advertising agency.

The first books that Aiken wrote, *All You've Ever Wanted* (1953) and *More Than*

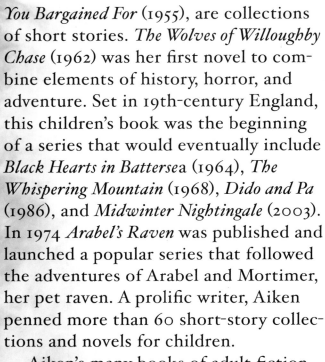

You Bargained For (1955), are collections of short stories. *The Wolves of Willoughby Chase* (1962) was her first novel to combine elements of history, horror, and adventure. Set in 19th-century England, this children's book was the beginning of a series that would eventually include *Black Hearts in Battersea* (1964), *The Whispering Mountain* (1968), *Dido and Pa* (1986), and *Midwinter Nightingale* (2003). In 1974 *Arabel's Raven* was published and launched a popular series that followed the adventures of Arabel and Mortimer, her pet raven. A prolific writer, Aiken penned more than 60 short-story collections and novels for children.

Aiken's many books of adult fiction, beginning with *The Silence of Herondale* (1964), are categorized as terror, suspense, and mystery stories. She also wrote a number of novels based on Jane Austen's works, including *Mansfield Revisited* (1984), *Jane Fairfax: Jane Austen's Emma Through Another's Eyes* (1990), and *Eliza's Daughter* (1994). Among Aiken's nonfiction works is *The Way to Write for Children* (1982). Aiken died on January 4, 2004, in Petworth, West Sussex.

V.C. ANDREWS

(b. 1923–d. 1986)

A wildly popular but critically panned author, V.C Andrews wrote gothic thrillers that explored the themes of female adolescence, abuse of power, revenge, social station, and the corruption of wealth.

Virginia Cleo Andrews was born in Portsmouth, Va. Readers often assume that her often sordid tales of dysfunctional families were based on her own life, but in fact she grew up in a stable household, the youngest of three children. Andrews fell down a flight of stairs when she was a teenager and suffered spinal injuries. Soon after she was diagnosed with rheumatoid arthritis. As a result of her accident and the disease, she was dependent on crutches and wheelchairs for most of her life.

As an adult, Andrews delivered on the artistic promise she showed early in life by working as a commercial artist and illustrator as an adult. In her spare time she wrote stories. Her first and most famous published work, *Flowers in the Attic* (1979; film 1987) was originally titled *The Obsessed*. The book,

a Gothic tale about four children abused by their grandmother, became a best-seller merely two weeks after its initial release.

Andrews was paid $7,500 for the rights to her first book. The next installment in the Dollanganger series (named after the *Flowers in the Attic* protagonists), *Petals on the Wind* (1980), earned her an advance of $35,000. Between the next two novels in the series, *If There Be Thorns* (1981) and *Seeds of Yesterday* (1984), Andrews wrote *My Sweet Audrina*, published in 1982. She subsequently wrote two books in her Casteel Family series, *Heaven* (1985), and *Dark Angel* (1986).

A final Dollanganger novel, *Garden of Shadows* (1987), was published after Andrews's death in 1986 from breast cancer. Several novels published under the V.C. Andrews name after her death are believed to have been based on synopses and notes left behind by Andrews herself.

AVI

(b. 1937–)

U.S. author Avi writes books that appeal to a young reader's sense of mystery and adventure. With more than 60 children's and young adult books under his belt, as well as a Newbery Medal and two Newbery Honor books, Avi has established himself as a notable author of children's literature.

Edward Irving Wortis was born in Brooklyn, N.Y., on Dec. 23, 1937. His twin sister started calling him Avi when they were young. As a child, Avi read as much as he could. He initially aspired to become an airplane designer, but several failing grades in high school science convinced him otherwise. Because of his poor academic performance, his parents transferred him to a small private school that offered additional help with reading and writing. Avi struggled his entire life with dysgraphia, a learning disability that affects spelling and handwriting. With the additional help he received, he came to enjoy writing and was determined to become a writer. He attended the University of Wisconsin at Madison and received his bachelor's degree in 1959 and his master's degree in 1962. Two years later he obtained a master's degree in library science from Columbia University.

Although Avi wrote numerous works of fiction, including animal stories, comedies, and fantasies, he is most famous for his

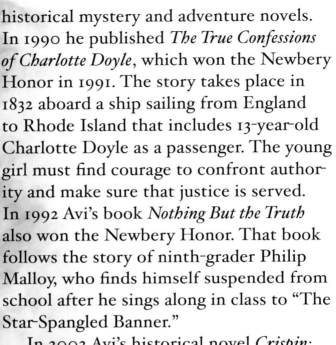

historical mystery and adventure novels. In 1990 he published *The True Confessions of Charlotte Doyle*, which won the Newbery Honor in 1991. The story takes place in 1832 aboard a ship sailing from England to Rhode Island that includes 13-year-old Charlotte Doyle as a passenger. The young girl must find courage to confront authority and make sure that justice is served. In 1992 Avi's book *Nothing But the Truth* also won the Newbery Honor. That book follows the story of ninth-grader Philip Malloy, who finds himself suspended from school after he sings along in class to "The Star-Spangled Banner."

In 2002 Avi's historical novel *Crispin: The Cross of Lead* was published. Orphaned and accused of a murder he did not commit, the book's title character sets off on a journey of self-discovery while attempting to avoid capture. The plot is enriched with lessons on feudalism and the injustices faced by the serf in 14th-century England. The book won the Newbery Medal in 2003. Crispin reappeared in an expanded series, which included *Crispin: At the Edge of the World* (2006) and *Crispin: The End of Time* (2010). Among Avi's other books were *Who Stole the Wizard of Oz?* (1981),

Poppy (1995), and *The Secret School* (2001). In addition to writing, Avi also worked as a librarian at the New York Public Library and Trenton State College.

CLIVE BARKER

(b. 1952–)

While accomplished as a director, visual artist, and playwright, Clive Barker is best known as a horror/fantasy novelist. His literary works reflect his passion for the *fantastique*, or dark fairy tale.

Barker was born in Liverpool, England, on Oct. 5, 1952. He went on to earn degrees in philosophy and English at the University of Liverpool while writing, directing, and acting in off-campus productions. His theatre troupe, the Dog Company, performed in London and Amsterdam from 1977 to 1983. It was during this period that he began writing novellas, which were published as *Books of Blood Vol.1* in 1984. Written during his spare time, on a rigorous regiment of 2,000 words per day, the series of graphically violent tales continued for five more installments.

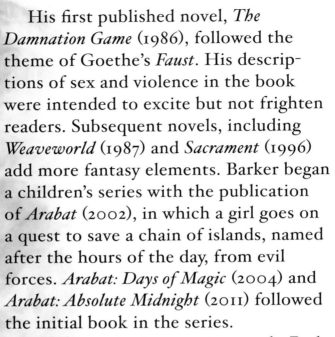

His first published novel, *The Damnation Game* (1986), followed the theme of Goethe's *Faust*. His descriptions of sex and violence in the book were intended to excite but not frighten readers. Subsequent novels, including *Weaveworld* (1987) and *Sacrament* (1996) add more fantasy elements. Barker began a children's series with the publication of *Arabat* (2002), in which a girl goes on a quest to save a chain of islands, named after the hours of the day, from evil forces. *Arabat: Days of Magic* (2004) and *Arabat: Absolute Midnight* (2011) followed the initial book in the series.

While continuing to write novels, Barker also developed a career as a screenwriter and director, most notably with *Hellraiser* (1987), based on his novella *The Hellbound Heart* (1986). Subsequent films based on his works have not been as commercially successful. As a producer, however, Barker achieved success with the film *Gods and Monsters* (1998).

Barker was also a painter and sketch artist, whose works have been shown in galleries and featured in his *Arabat* series of books. He also has dabbled in computer games (*Clive Barker's Undying*, 2001) and comic book adaptations of *Hellraiser*, including *The Harrowers* and *Book of the Damned*.

AMBROSE BIERCE

(b. 1842–d. 1914)

Ambrose Bierce was an American newspaperman and satirist who also wrote short stories based on themes of death and horror. Fittingly, his life ended in an unsolved mystery.

Ambrose Gwinnett Bierce was born in Ohio and raised in Indiana. He became a printer's apprentice on a newspaper after about a year in high school. In 1861 he enlisted in the 9th Indiana Volunteers and fought in a number of American Civil War battles, including Shiloh and Chickamauga. After being seriously wounded in the Battle of Kennesaw Mountain in 1864, he served until January 1865, and he received a merit promotion to major in 1867.

Resettling in San Francisco after the war, Bierce began contributing to periodicals, particularly the *News Letter*, of which he became editor in 1868. His first fiction story, *The Haunted Valley*, was published in

Portrait of Ambrose Bierce, whose mysterious death could have been a plotline in one of his horror tales. Library of Congress Prints and Photographs Division

1871. In December of that year he married Mary Ellen Day, and from 1872 to 1875 the Bierces lived in England. During that time he wrote for the London magazines *Fun* and *Figaro* and published three books, *The Fiend's Delight* (1872), *Nuggets and Dust Panned Out in California* (1872), and *Cobwebs from an Empty Skull* (1874).

The couple returned to the United States, where Bierce worked as an editor and columnist for a number of newspapers, punctuated by a brief, unsuccessful stint as a miner in the Dakota Territory in the late 1870s.

Bierce's principal works of fiction are *In the Midst of Life* (1892), which includes some of his finest stories, such as "An Occurrence at Owl Creek Bridge," "A Horseman in the Sky," "The Eyes of the Panther," and "The Boarded Window;" and *Can Such Things Be?* (1893), which includes "The Damned Thing" and "Moxon's Master." Bierce's *The Devil's Dictionary* (originally published in 1906 as *The Cynic's Word Book*) is a volume of ironic, even bitter, definitions of common words. (*The Enlarged Devil's Dictionary*, edited by E.J. Hopkins, appeared in 1967 and was reprinted in 2001.) His *Collected Works* was published in 12 volumes, 1909–12.

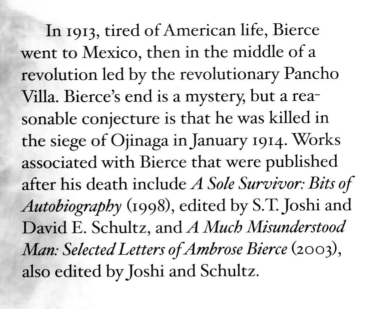

In 1913, tired of American life, Bierce went to Mexico, then in the middle of a revolution led by the revolutionary Pancho Villa. Bierce's end is a mystery, but a reasonable conjecture is that he was killed in the siege of Ojinaga in January 1914. Works associated with Bierce that were published after his death include *A Sole Survivor: Bits of Autobiography* (1998), edited by S.T. Joshi and David E. Schultz, and *A Much Misunderstood Man: Selected Letters of Ambrose Bierce* (2003), also edited by Joshi and Schultz.

ROBERT ALBERT BLOCH

(b. 1917–d. 1994)

R obert Albert Bloch crafted dozens of screenplays, mysteries, fantasies, and essays. Yet he was best remembered for his spine-tingling psychological tales of horror and suspense, most notably the classic *Psycho* (1959), a cult favorite that was adapted for Alfred Hitchcock's 1960 film of the same title.

Bloch was born in Chicago, Ill., on April 5, 1917. He worked for an advertising agency while writing stories for the magazine *Weird Tales*. In his stories, he relied on elements of surprise rather than scenes of graphic violence or mythological forces to terrorize and captivate readers. He was also one of the first writers to delve into the criminal mind. His style, which was influenced by the writings of his mentor, H.P. Lovecraft, was also the model for horror specialist Stephen King and science-fiction writer Ray Bradbury.

In 1953, Bloch quit his job at the advertising agency to become a full-time writer. After publishing his first novel, *The Scarf* (1947), he began a prolific career writing for television, radio, and film. Some of his screenplays include *Torture Garden* (1967), *The House That Dripped Blood* (1970), and *Asylum* (1972). In addition to his tales of horror and suspense for the screen, Bloch also wrote 39 episodes for the radio program *Stay Tuned for Terror* and established his reputation through multiple broadcasts and republications of the story "Yours Truly, Jack the Ripper." Bloch died on Sept. 23, 1994, in Los Angeles, Calif.

ANTHONY BOUCHER

(b. 1911–d. 1968)

American Anthony Boucher made a name for himself as an author, editor, and critic in the mystery and science fiction genres. In 1949, he cofounded the *Magazine of Fantasy & Science Fiction*, a major science fiction periodical. In addition, he was one of the premier critics of mystery; for his reviews he won three Edgar Allan Poe Awards (1946, 1950, and 1953) from the Mystery Writers of America.

His given name was William Anthony Parker White; Boucher was a pseudonym, or pen name. Boucher was born on Aug. 21, 1911, in Oakland, Calif. He wrote his first novel, the mystery *The Case of the Seven of Cavalry*, in 1937. Boucher sold his first science fiction story, *Snulbug*, to the magazine *Unknown* in 1941.

Three of Boucher's novels and several of his short stories featured Fergus O'Breen, a private detective whose cases involved supernatural and science-fictional elements such as werewolves and time travel. Boucher's Roman Catholicism surfaced in the character of Sister Ursula, a crime-solving nun who appeared in two novels that Boucher wrote under another pseudonym, H.H. Holmes. *Rocket to the Morgue* (1942), a Sister Ursula novel, featured thinly veiled portraits of science fiction writers such as Robert Heinlein and L. Ron Hubbard.

From 1945 to 1948, Boucher wrote scripts for several nationally broadcast radio mystery series. Beginning in the 1940s, he reviewed mysteries and science fiction for the the *New York Times* and other American newspapers.

In 1949 he and author J. Francis McComas founded the *Magazine of Fantasy & Science Fiction* (*F&SF*), which aimed to publish work at a higher literary level than had previously existed in the genre. *F&SF* encouraged a new generation of science fiction authors that included Philip K. Dick and Alfred Bester. After McComas left *F&SF* in 1954, Boucher edited the magazine alone until 1958. He also reviewed operas for *Opera News* in the 1960s.

The annual world mystery convention, Bouchercon, first held in 1970, is named in his honor. Boucher died in Oakland on April 29, 1968.

DAN BROWN

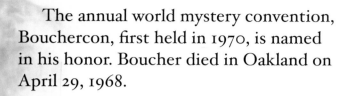

(b. 1964–)

American author Dan Brown writes well-researched novels that center on secret organizations and have intricate plots. He is best known for the Robert Langdon series, which notably includes *The Da Vinci Code* (2003).

Brown was born June 22, 1964, in Exeter, N.H. He attended Phillips Exeter Academy, a prep school where his father was a math teacher, and in 1986 he graduated from Amherst (Massachusetts) College. He then moved to California to pursue a career as a songwriter, to little success. In 1990 he wrote his first book, *187 Men to Avoid*, a dating survival guide for women that was published in 1995.

In 1993 Brown joined the faculty at Exeter as an English and creative-writing teacher. Several years later the U.S. Secret Service

Author Dan Brown poses in front of a sign promoting the movie based on his best-selling *The Da Vinci Code* while on his way to the film's premiere in Cannes, France, in 2006. Getty Images

visited the school to interview a student who had written an e-mail in which he joked about killing the president. The incident sparked Brown's interest in covert intelligence agencies, which formed the basis of his first novel, *Digital Fortress* (1998). Centered on secret organizations and code breaking, the novel became a model for Brown's later works.

In his next novel, *Angels & Demons* (2000), Brown introduced Robert Langdon, a Harvard professor of symbology, which involves interpreting symbols. The fast-paced thriller follows Langdon's attempts to protect the Vatican from the Illuminati, a secret society formed during the Renaissance that opposed the Roman Catholic Church. Although the novel received positive reviews, it failed to catch on with readers.

After his third novel, *Deception Point* (2001), Brown returned to Langdon with *The Da Vinci Code*, a thriller that centers on art history, Christianity's origins, and mysterious theories. Attempting to solve the murder of the Louvre's curator, Langdon encounters secret organizations (Opus Dei and the Priory of Sion), discusses the hidden messages in Leonardo da Vinci's art, raises the possibility that Jesus married Mary Magdelene and fathered a child, and discovers the Holy Grail.

Although controversial, especially among those who study religions, *The Da Vinci Code* proved immensely popular with readers. By 2009 more than 80 million copies had been sold, and editions were available in some 40 languages. Intense interest in the novel resulted in a spate of *Code*-related books and sparked sales of Brown's earlier works; in 2004 all four of his novels appeared simultaneously on the *New York Times* best-seller lists. The film adaptations of *The Da Vinci Code* and *Angels & Demons* were released in 2006 and 2009, respectively, with Tom Hanks starring as Langdon. Brown continued the adventures of his protagonist in *The Lost Symbol* (2009), which centers on Freemasons, and *Inferno* (2013), which saw Langdon following clues related to Dante's poem *The Divine Comedy* in an effort to stop the release of a plague.

JAMES M. CAIN

(b. 1892–d. 1977)

Novelist James M. Cain wrote violent, sexually obsessed, and relentlessly paced melodramas that epitomized the hard-boiled school of writing that flourished in the United States in the 1930s and 1940s. Three of his novels—*The Postman Always Rings Twice* (1934), *Double Indemnity* (1936), and *Mildred Pierce* (1941)—were also made into classics of the American screen.

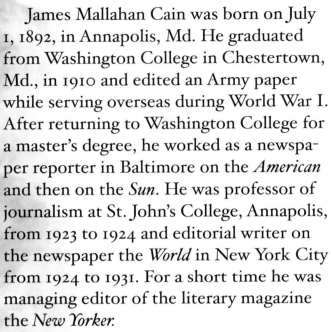

James Mallahan Cain was born on July 1, 1892, in Annapolis, Md. He graduated from Washington College in Chestertown, Md., in 1910 and edited an Army paper while serving overseas during World War I. After returning to Washington College for a master's degree, he worked as a newspaper reporter in Baltimore on the *American* and then on the *Sun*. He was professor of journalism at St. John's College, Annapolis, from 1923 to 1924 and editorial writer on the newspaper the *World* in New York City from 1924 to 1931. For a short time he was managing editor of the literary magazine the *New Yorker.*

His first novel, *The Postman Always Rings Twice*, published when he was 42 years old, was a spectacular success. Its sordid environment, characters that seek to gain their ends through violence, and taut, fast-paced writing style set the pattern for most of his later books. *Serenade* (1937) was daring for its time in its presentation of a bisexual hero. *Three of a Kind* (1943) contained the short novels *Career in C Major*, *Double Indemnity* (which had previously been published in a serial version), and *The Embezzler*. His books continued to appear after World War II—among them *The Butterfly* (1947), *The*

Moth (1948), *The Root of His Evil* (1954), *The Magician's Wife* (1965), *and Rainbow's End* (1975)—but none were as successful as his earlier works. Cain died on Oct. 27, 1977, in University Park, Md.

JULIE CAMPBELL

(b. 1908–d. 1999)

American author Julie Campbell wrote books for young adults. She is best known for writing the first six books of the *Trixie Belden* mystery series.

Born into a military family in Flushing, N.Y., on June 1, 1908, Campbell spent her childhood living in various locations. While living in Hawaii, she won a short story contest at the age of eight. She spent years working in journalism and business before opening her own literary agency in the 1940s. She was approached by Western Publishing to conceive a series of children's mystery books, and responded to the call with four ideas, two of which she would write herself.

Over a ten-year period, starting in 1948, Campbell wrote six *Trixie Belden* books. Set in the fictional town of Sleepyside, the series centered on the thirteen-year-old heroine after whom the series is named and her group of friends who band together to solve mysteries. Many of the book's characters and settings were inspired by Campbell's own life in her hometown near Ossining, N.Y. She got many of her plots from newspaper articles.

After the publication of her sixth *Trixie Belden* book, *Trixie Belden and the Mystery in Arizona* (1958), Campbell wished to end the series, but faced protest from her publishers. A deal was struck in which Campbell, as the creator of the characters, would receive royalties from the six subsequent titles. Thereafter, the series was published under the pseudonym Kathryn Kenny. Campbell reportedly never consulted with any of the *Trixie Belden* authors who succeeded her.

In addition to the Trixie Belden books, Campbell wrote a total of eighteen books for three other mystery series. The protagonists for those series were nurse Cherry Ames, whose books were extremely popular in their day; Ginny Gordon, who was very similar to Trixie Belden in age and sleuthing; and stewardess (now called flight attendant) and amateur detective Vicki Barr. Campbell also wrote several stand-alone novels during this period as well, including *The Mongrel of Merryway Farm* (1952) and *To Nick from Jan* (1957). She died on July 7, 1999, in Alexandria, Va.

RAYMOND CHANDLER

(b. 1888–d. 1959)

Raymond Chandler was a well-known author of detective fiction. Most notably he was the creator of the private detective Philip Marlowe, a poor but honest upholder of ideals living and working in Los Angeles, Calif.

Raymond Thornton Chandler was born in Chicago, Ill., on July 23, 1888. From 1896 to 1912 he lived in England with his mother, a British subject of Irish birth. Although he was an American citizen and a resident of California when World War I began in 1914, he served in the Canadian army and then in the Royal Flying Corps (afterward the Royal Air Force).

Mystery writer Raymond Chandler, the creator of fictional detective Philip Marlowe. Ralph Crane/Time & Life Pictures/ Getty Images

Having returned to California in 1919, Chandler did well financially as a petroleum company executive until the Great Depression of the 1930s, when he turned to writing for a living. His first published short story appeared in the pulp magazine *Black Mask* in 1933. Chandler completed seven novels, all with Philip Marlowe as hero: *The Big Sleep* (1939), *Farewell, My Lovely* (1940), *The High Window* (1942), *The Lady in the Lake* (1943), *The Little Sister* (1949), *The Long Goodbye* (1953), and *Playback* (1958).

From 1943 on Chandler worked as a Hollywood screenwriter. Among his best-known scripts were those for the films *Double Indemnity* (1944), *The Blue Dahlia* (1946), and *Strangers on a Train* (1951), the last written in collaboration with Czenzi Ormonde.

Among his numerous short-story collections are *Five Murderers* (1944) and *The Midnight Raymond Chandler* (1971). The most popular film versions of Chandler's work were *Murder, My Sweet* (1944; also distributed as *Farewell, My Lovely*), starring Dick Powell, and *The Big Sleep* (1946), starring Humphrey Bogart. Both movies are considered film noir classics.

AGATHA CHRISTIE

(b. 1890–d. 1976)

Most of English detective novelist and playwright Agatha Christie's approximately 75 novels became best-sellers; translated into 100 languages, they have sold more than 100 million copies.

Christie was born Agatha Miller on Sept. 15, 1890, in Devon, England. Educated at home by her mother, Christie began writing detective fiction while working as a nurse during World War I. The publication of her first novel, *The Mysterious Affair at Styles* (1920), introduced the world to Hercule Poirot, one of the most famous of all names in detective fiction. Her other famous detective, Miss Jane Marple, first appeared in *Murder at the Vicarage* (1930).

Christie's plays include *The Mousetrap* (1952), which set a world record for the longest continuous run at one theater, and *Witness for the Prosecution* (1953); the latter was adapted to the silver screen in 1958). Other notable film adaptations of Christie's stories include *Murder on the*

Dame Agatha Christie, posing with handwritten notes, at her Devonshire home in the 1940s. AFP/Getty Images

Orient Express (1933; film, 1974) and *Death on the Nile* (1937; film, 1978). Her works were also adapted for television.

Her 1914 marriage to Col. Archibald Christie ended in divorce in 1928. In 1930 she married archaeologist Sir Max Mallowan. She spent several months each year on expeditions in Iraq and Syria with him. In addition to her detective fiction, she also wrote romantic nondetective novels, such as *Absent in the Spring* (1944), under the pseudonym Mary Westmacott.

Christie was created a Dame of the British Empire in 1971. She died at Wallingford in Oxfordshire on Jan. 12, 1976. Her *Autobiography* (1977) appeared posthumously.

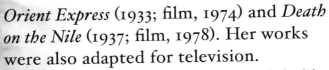

TOM CLANCY

(b. 1947–d. 2013)

U.S. author Tom Clancy began his working life as an insurance broker, but ultimately found success as the author of best-selling thrillers. Although he never served in the military himself, he created the genre of military thrillers.

Born in 1947 in Baltimore, Md., Thomas Clancy broke onto the writing scene with *The Hunt for Red October*, which made several best-seller lists for the novice writer. *Red October* is credited with popularizing the "technothriller" genre—suspenseful novels that rely on extensive knowledge of military technology and espionage. The book was made into a film in 1990, starring Sean Connery and Alec Baldwin.

Clancy's second book, *Red Storm Rising* (1986), was also a best-seller. It was followed in quick succession by *Patriot Games* (1987; film, 1992), *The Cardinal in the Kremlin* (1988), and *Clear and Present Danger* (1989; film, 1994). His literary output in the 1990s included *The Sum of All Fears* (1991; film, 2002), *Without Remorse* (1993), *Debt of Honor* (1994), *Executive Orders* (1996), and *Rainbow Six* (1998), which also served as the basis for a line of video games. The 21st century saw the publication of *The Bear and the Dragon* (2000) and *The Teeth of the Tiger* (2003).

Clancy's nonfiction works include *Into the Storm: A Study in Command* (1997; 2nd ed., 2007), cowritten with Fred Franks, Jr.,

and *Every Man a Tiger* (1999; updated ed., 2005), cowritten with Chuck Horner.

Clancy died in Baltimore, Md. on Oct. 1, 2013.

MARY HIGGINS CLARK

(b. 1929–)

Mary Higgins Clark has written several best-selling stories that chill the spine and entertain readers both young and old. She has been called "The Queen of Suspense."

Born in Bronx, N.Y. on Dec. 24, 1929, Mary Theresa Eleanor Higgins was raised by a single mother after her father died when she was eleven years old. After her high school graduation, she worked for several years as a secretary at an advertising agency, then as a flight attendant with Pan American Airlines. In 1950 she married Warren Clark; they had five children. She sold her first short story, titled "Stowaway," to *Extension Magazine* in 1956.

Widowed in 1964, Clark earned money to support her family by writing scripts for radio programs. As a sideline, she tried her hand at writing books as well. Her first published book, *Aspire to the Heavens* (1969; reissued in 2002 as *Mount Vernon Love Story*), was a fictionalized account of the life of George Washington. Her first fiction novel, the thriller *Where Are the Children?* (1975; film, 1986), zoomed to the top of best-seller lists.

Among the more than two dozen suspense novels penned by Higgins Clark were *A Stranger Is Watching* (1978; film, 1982), *The Cradle Will Fall* (1980), *I'll Be Seeing You* (1993), *On the Street Where You Live* (2001), and *Daddy's Gone A Hunting* (2013). Along with her daughter Carol Higgins Clark, she has co-authored a series of holiday-themed suspense novels, including *Deck the Halls* (2000) and *The Christmas Thief* (2004). Many of Mary Higgins Clark's numerous short stories are compiled in three collections: *The Anastasia Syndrome & Other Stories* (1989), *The Lottery Winner: Alvirah & Willy Stories* (1994), and *My Gal Sunday: Henry and Sunday Stories* (1996).

In addition to the theatrical releases of *Where Are the Children?* and *A Stranger Is Watching*, television films have been made based on several of her short stories and novels. In 2002, she published a memoir, *Kitchen Privileges.*

In 1987, Higgins Clark served as president of Mystery Writers of America, the same organization that created an annual award named in her honor.

WILKIE COLLINS

(b. 1842–d. 1889)

O ne of the first and greatest masters of the mystery story, Wilkie Collins was the first British novelist to write in this genre. He was a much-imitated writer: the motif of *The Moonstone* (1868), concerning a cursed jewel that was originally stolen from an idol's eye, has been repeated countless times, and his Count Fosco in *The Woman in White* (1860) is the original of innumerable bravura villains.

William Wilkie Collins, the son of landscape painter William Collins, was born on Jan. 8, 1824, in London, England. He developed a gift for inventing tales while still a schoolboy at a private boarding school. At an early age he was placed in the tea trade, where his performance was undistinguished.

After studying law at Lincoln's Inn, he was admitted to the bar in 1851 but proved to have as little aptitude for law as for commerce. He worked, instead, on a historical novel, painted well enough to have a picture hung at the Royal Academy, engaged in theatricals, and visited Paris, France.

His first published work was a memoir of his father, who died in 1847, *Memoirs of the Life of William Collins, Esq., R.A.* (1848). His fiction followed shortly after: *Antonina; or, the Fall of Rome* (1850) and *Basil* (1852), a highly colored tale of seduction and vengeance with a contemporary middle-class setting and passages of uncompromising realism. In 1851 he began an association with Charles Dickens that exerted a formative influence on his career. Their admiration was mutual. Under Dickens's influence, Collins developed a talent for characterization, humor, and popular success, while the older writer's debt to Collins is evident in the more skillful and suspenseful plot structures of such novels as *A Tale of Two Cities* (1859) and *Great Expectations* (1860–61). Collins began contributing serials to Dickens's periodical *Household Words*, and his first major work, *The Woman in White*, appeared in Dickens's *All the Year Round*.

Among Collins's most successful subsequent books were *No Name* (1862) and *Armadale* (1866). *The Moonstone* is often considered one of the best detective stories ever written. Besides being one of the first novels to be built wholly around an ingenious plot (the formula that is used in the modern mystery story), it also cleverly uses letter exchanges among characters to advance the story. Collins died on Sept. 23, 1889, in London.

RICHARD THOMAS CONDON

(b. 1915–d. 1996)

American Richard Thomas Condon began his career as a writer after years as a publicist. His best-known novel is *The Manchurian Candidate*.

Condon was born and educated in New York City. After graduating from DeWitt Clinton High School, he worked as an elevator operator, hotel clerk, and a waiter. He began a career in the film industry in the 1930s, working as a studio publicist for

Twentieth Century Fox, the Walt Disney Studios, and others. Based in New York, his job entailed, in his words, "pimping" for visiting movie stars. While still working in publicity, he sold a short story to *Esquire* magazine and wrote a play, *Men of Distinction* (1953), which made it to Broadway but closed after only four performances.

Undeterred by the play's lack of success, Condon quit the publicity business in 1957 to become a full-time writer. His first novel, *The Oldest Confession*, was published a year later. His second novel, *The Manchurian Candidate* (1959; films 1962, 2004) was a tale of government conspiracy gone wrong. The themes of the novel were a reflection of his personal traits: cynical, mistrustful of government and large corporations, and contemptuous of politicians and men in powerful positions.

Condon made no secret of his particular distaste of American politics. Several of his novels, including *The Vertical Smile* (1971), *The Star Spangled Crunch* (1974), and *The Final Addiction* (1991) are thinly veiled attacks on former American presidents.

Condon turned his critical eye towards the Mafia, and America's fascination with it, in *Prizzi's Honor* (1982), a book about a hit man who falls in love with his female counter-part in a rival crime family. A successful film adaptation (1982) starring Jack Nicholson and directed by John Huston earned Condon an Academy Award nomination (with cowriter Janet Roach) for Best Adapted Screenplay. Other Prizzi books include the prequel *Prizzi's Family* (1986) and sequels *Prizzi's Glory* (1988) and *Prizzi's Money* (1994). Condon died in Dallas on April 9, 1996.

PATRICIA CORNWELL

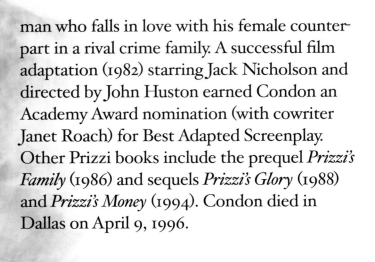

(b. 1956–)

C rime thrillers are the preferred sub-genre of writer Patricia Cornwell. She is best known for her best-selling series featuring the medical examiner Dr. Kay Scarpetta.

Born Patricia Carroll Daniels on June 9, 1956, in Miami, Fla., Patricia grew up in North Carolina. Her father deserted the family when she was five years old. Several years later her depressed mother attempted to give the girl away to neighbors, the Baptist evangelist Billy Graham and his wife, Ruth. Daniels stayed with friends of the Grahams while her mother recovered from a nervous breakdown. These child-hood experiences left their mark. During her years at Davidson College (B.A., 1979) in North Carolina, she fought eating dis-orders and was admitted for a brief stay in a mental hospital. She married one of her professors, Charles Cornwell, in 1979. (The couple divorced a decade later.)

After graduating Patricia Cornwell took a job as a police reporter for the *Charlotte Observer.* Because her career brought her into close contact with many aspects of crime, she strove to understand all the intri-cacies and facets of criminal behavior. She volunteered as a police officer, spent endless hours in the morgue's medical library, and took classes in forensic science at the police academy. She also interviewed medical examiners and worked at the office of the chief medical examiner in Richmond, Va., where she was allowed to observe autopsies.

Cornwell's first book, *A Time for Remembering* (1983), was a biography of Ruth Graham. She made the focus of her second book crime. Her first three essays in the crime novel genre had been rejected by publishers, but she was encouraged by one editor to develop the fictional character of Kay Scarpetta, who had appeared in minor roles in the early attempts. Scarpetta—who was much like Cornwell in appearance, thought, and deed—was featured as a medical examiner in *Postmortem* (1990), the book that launched Cornwell's writing career. The novel was the first to win five literary awards in one year.

The Scarpetta series continued with *Body of Evidence* (1991), *All That Remains* (1992), *Cause of Death* (1996), *Black Notice* (1999), *Blow Fly* (2003), *Book of the Dead* (2007), *Scarpetta* (2008), *The Scarpetta Factor* (2009), *Port Mortuary* (2010), *Red Mist* (2011), *The Bone Bed* (2012), and *Dust* (2013). Early efforts in the series maintained a first-person voice, allowing the reader insight into the mind of the keenly observant Scarpetta. Several later novels employed third-person narration. Cornwell used the latter approach to explore the disturbed minds of the criminals the protagonist sought, but eventually returned to using Scarpetta's perspective alone.

The novels developed an intense following, selling more than 100 million copies.

Cornwell is the recipient of a number of awards crime thriller and literary awards. Her character Kay Scarpetta was the winner of the Sherlock Award in 1999, named the best detective created by an American author that year.

Cornwell ventured into other genres with the general fiction novel *Isle of Dogs* (2001); a children's book, *Life's Little Fable* (1999); and a work of nonfiction titled *Portrait of a Killer: Jack the Ripper—Case Closed* (2002). The latter book was the object of controversy over Cornwell's theory that the artist Walter Sickert was the infamous killer.

MICHAEL CRICHTON

(b. 1942–d. 2008)

Michael Crichton was known as the "father of the techno-thriller." Crichton drew an enormous following with his novels, movie screenplays, and the TV series *ER*. His novel *Jurassic Park* topped best-seller lists, and its movie adaptation broke box-office records

and fueled the world's fascination with dinosaurs.

John Michael Crichton was born in Chicago on Oct. 23, 1942, the oldest of four children. His parents, John Henderson Crichton and Zula Miller Crichton, moved the family to the Long Island town of Roslyn, N.Y., when Michael was six.

Doctor-turned-author Michael Crichton at a 2002 book signing event in Century City, Calif. Frederick M. Brown/ Getty Images

Crichton's father was an executive and journalist for *Advertising Age*, and Michael showed an early aptitude for writing. His first published piece, a travel article, appeared in the *New York Times* when he was only 14. He wanted to become a writer, but his papers routinely earned C-minus grades at Harvard University, where he received his undergraduate degree. Feeling that the fault lay with the school and not with himself, Crichton decided to turn in an essay written by the noted British writer George Orwell. When the professor gave the essay a B-minus Crichton switched his English major to anthropology. He took the classes required for medical school, graduated summa cum laude and Phi Beta Kappa, and at age 23 traveled to England's Cambridge University as a visiting lecturer in anthropology. He also won a Henry Russell Shaw Fellowship and traveled in Europe and Northern Africa.

In 1965 Crichton returned to the United States to enter Harvard Medical School, where he earned a medical degree in 1969. As a medical student Crichton wrote spy thrillers under the pseudonyms John Lange and Jeffrey Hudson to help pay his tuition.

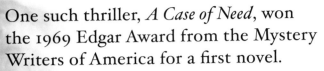

One such thriller, *A Case of Need*, won the 1969 Edgar Award from the Mystery Writers of America for a first novel.

Crichton's first best-seller, *The Andromeda Strain*, was published in 1969 under his own name, and he sold the movie rights to Hollywood. Two years later, he published his first nonfiction piece, *Five Patients: The Hospital Explained*, which was based on his research and experiences as a medical student. Crichton was named the 1970 medical writer of the year by the Association of American Medical Writers for *Five Patients*. At the Jonas Salk Institute for Biological Science in La Jolla, Calif., Crichton served as a postdoctoral fellow in 1969 and 1970. However, he had already decided to pursue a writing career and, after visiting the movie set of *The Andromeda Strain*, he gave up his medical career entirely.

Crichton produced three more novels in the 1970s—*The Terminal Man* (1972), *The Great Train Robbery* (1972), and *Eaters of the Dead* (1976)—as well as a biography of contemporary artist Jasper Johns (1977). He won another Edgar Award in 1980 for *The Great Train Robbery*. Two more novels, *Congo* and *Sphere*, were published in 1980 and 1987, respectively.

In 1990 Crichton published the massively successful science fiction thriller *Jurassic Park*. Three years later it was made into a motion picture. Many of his works were translated to screenplays. In addition, Crichton wrote the screenplays for and directed *Westworld* (1973), *Coma* (1978), and *The Great Train Robbery* (1979).

Crichton's first taste of negative publicity came in 1992 with the publication of *Rising Sun*, a story of Japanese-American relations and technological warfare that some criticized as anti-Japanese. Some criticism continued with the publication of *Disclosure*, a book about a woman who sexually harasses a male coworker. In 1995 Crichton returned to safer ground with the publication of *The Lost World*, a sequel to *Jurassic Park*. The next year, he cowrote the screenplay for the movie *Twister* and published a novel about the airline industry and the media, *Airframe*. The movie version of *The Lost World* came out in 1997 and drew more throngs to the theaters.

In addition to his success in bookstores and movie theaters, Crichton created and produced the hit television series *ER*, a weekly hour-long drama about crises and relationships in a hospital emergency room. In 1995 *ER* won eight Emmy Awards, and Crichton himself received honors from the Producers Guild of America, as well as winning the George Foster Peabody Award for the series.

An avid traveler, Crichton described many of his adventures in the autobiographical *Travels* (1988). He also operated a computer software company, FilmTrack, for a short period and produced the computer game *Amazon*. Some of Crichton's later works include *Prey* (2002), *State of Fear* (2005), and *Next* (2006). He died of cancer on Nov. 4, 2008, in Los Angeles.

ARTHUR CONAN DOYLE

(b. 1859–d. 1930)

A Scottish physician who turned to writing, Arthur Conan Doyle thought he would be remembered for his historical novels. His fame, however, rests on his creation of the master detective of fiction, the incomparable Sherlock Holmes.

Arthur Conan Doyle was born in Edinburgh, Scotland, on May 22, 1859. He was the oldest son of Charles Doyle, a civil servant. His parents were Irish Roman Catholics, and he received his early education in a Jesuit school, Stonyhurst. Later he got a medical degree at Edinburgh University. He started practice as a family physician in Southsea, England. His income was small so he began writing stories to make ends meet. In 1891 he decided to give up medicine to concentrate on his writing.

A Study in Scarlet, published in 1887, introduced Holmes and his friend Dr. John Watson. The second Holmes story was *The Sign of Four* (1890). In 1891 Doyle began a series for *Strand* magazine called "The Adventures of Sherlock Holmes." Sherlock Holmes became known to movie and television audiences as a tall and lean, pipe-smoking, violin-playing detective. He lived at 221B Baker Street in London, where he was often visited by Watson, an associate in the many adventures. And

Sir Arthur Conan Doyle, the author who wrote stories featuring the immensely popular detective Sherlock Holmes. Encyclopædia Britannica, Inc.

according to Doyle, it was Watson who recorded the Holmes stories for posterity.

Doyle said he modeled Holmes after one of his teachers in Edinburgh, Dr. Joseph Bell. Bell could, for example, glance at a corpse on the anatomy table and deduce that the person had been a left-handed shoemaker. "It is all very well to say that a man is clever," Doyle wrote, "but the reader wants to see examples of it—such examples as Bell gave us every day in the wards." The author eventually became bored with Holmes and "killed" him. In response to readers' protests, Doyle wrote his next story explaining how the detective had miraculously survived the death struggle on the edge of a precipice. Stories dealing with Holmes's exploits continued to appear almost to the end of Doyle's life.

Doyle was knighted in 1902 for his pamphlet justifying England's part in the Boer War, in which he served at a field hospital. He was married twice. The death of his son Kingsley in World War I intensified Doyle's interest in psychic phenomena; in his later years he wrote and lectured on spiritualism. He died in Sussex on July 7, 1930.

JANET EVANOVICH

(b. 1943–)

American novelist Janet Evanovich started out writing romance novels, but she is equally well-known for her mystery writing. She is the author of a series of books featuring hapless, smart-mouthed New Jersey bounty hunter Stephanie Plum.

She was born Janet Schneider and was raised in a working-class family in South River, New Jersey. She studied painting at Rutgers University's Douglass College, graduating with a bachelor's degree in 1965. Having married mathematician Peter Evanovich the previous year, she joined him on his travels around the country while he worked for the U.S. Navy. She became a homemaker following the births of her two children.

During her time home with the children, she began writing stories—many of them erotic—and submitting them for publication. After a decade of unsuccessful efforts to publish her tales, Evanovich had one of her romance novels accepted by Berkley Books for its Second Chance at Love imprint. The book was published as *Hero at Large* in 1987 under the pseudonym Steffie

Hall. Evanovich subsequently churned out nearly a dozen similarly themed books before growing restive and turning an eye toward the mystery genre.

While looking for a mystery concept, Evanovich viewed the film *Midnight Run* (1988), which starred Robert DeNiro as a bounty hunter. Intrigued, she spent two years researching bail bondsmen and law enforcement before setting to work on the story that became *One for the Money* (1994; television movie, 2002; film, 2012). Later entries in the cheeky series chronicled heroine Stephanie Plum's further attempts to track down criminals, often while juggling romantic crises.

The Stephanie Plum series has continued to grow in popularity, and ensuing volumes—among them *Hot Six* (2000), *Twelve Sharp* (2006), and *Notorious Nineteen* (2012)—became fixtures on the *New York Times* best-seller list. *Takedown Twenty* was scheduled for publication in 2013. Evanovich also wrote several novels featuring her bail bondsman crime-stopper, collected in a series referred to as "Between the Numbers" novels: *Visions of Sugar Plums* (2002), *Plum Lovin'* (2007), *Plum Lucky* (2008), and *Plum Spooky* (2009).

Author Janet Evanovich (left) poses with actress Katherine Heigel at the New York City premiere of One for the Money, in 2012. Gary Gershoff/WireImage/ Getty Images

Evanovich's winning formula—a sharp-tongued female protagonist aided in her madcap adventures by a smoldering, unavailable man and a cadre of eccentrics—proved so successful that she deployed it with only minor variations in her other series. Her mysteries set in the NASCAR scene—including *Metro Girl* (2004) and *Motor Mouth* (2006)—featured mechanic Alexandra Barnaby working alongside NASCAR driver Sam Hooker; the pair also appeared in several graphic novels. Evanovich's supernatural mysteries, including *Wicked Appetite* (2010) and *Wicked Business* (2012), featured pastry chef Elizabeth Tucker and mysterious, supernaturally gifted Diesel, who first appeared in the Plum holiday novels.

Evanovich continued to write romances (with a coauthor), among them *The Husband List* (2013; with Dorien Kelly). Additionally, she purchased the rights to her early efforts in the romance genre and sold them to another publishing company. She also penned a writer's guide, *How I Write: Secrets of a Bestselling Author* (2006; with Ina Yalof). Evanovich was the director and president of Evanovich, Inc., a company created to manage her output and publicity; it employed her husband and both of her children.

IAN FLEMING

(b. 1908–d. 1964)

Arguably the best-known hero of spy fiction in the late 20th century is James Bond, the creation of British novelist Ian Fleming. The Bond books have sold by the millions, and several of them have been made into popular motion pictures.

Fleming was born in London on May 28, 1908, and educated in England, Germany, and Switzerland. After his schooling he worked as a journalist in Moscow from 1929 to 1933 and as a banker and stockbroker from 1935 to 1939. During World War II he was an officer in British naval intelligence. He returned to journalism after the war as foreign manager of the London *Sunday Times*.

The first of the Bond stories, *Casino Royale*, was published in 1953. It was followed by 12 more Bond novels: *Live and Let Die* (1954), *Moonraker* (1955), *Diamonds Are Forever*, (1956), *From Russia with Love* (1957),

Doctor No (1958), *Goldfinger* (1959), *For Your Eyes Only* (1960), *Thunderball* (1961), *The Spy Who Loved Me* (1962), *On Her Majesty's Secret Service* (1963), *You Only Live Twice* (1964), and *The Man with the Golden Gun* (posthumously, 1965). Set in the world of international

British author Ian Fleming, looking every bit as dapper as his famous protagonist, James Bond. Express/Hulton Archive/Getty Images

espionage, these novels are filled with violence, romance, narrow escapes, complicated intrigue, and technological wizardry. Bond became the epitome of the playboy-hero of the 1950s and 1960s—cool, shrewd, tough, and irresistible to the incredible number of beautiful women who briefly passed in and out of his exciting life.

Ian Fleming died in Canterbury, England, on Aug. 12, 1964, at the height of his success. Attempts have been made by other authors to revive the Bond stories, but their books have not met with the same popular acclaim.

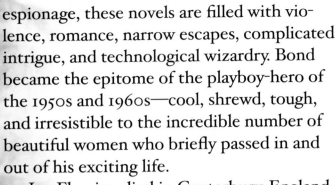

KEN FOLLETT

(b. 1949–)

During his youth, author Ken Follett was not permitted to watch television or listen to the radio, so he turned to books for entertainment. He credits being able to check books out of the public library for his talent as a writer.

Follett was born in Cardiff, Wales, on June 5, 1949, to a conservative Christian family. He graduated from University College in London with a degree in philosophy and became a reporter for the *South Wales Echo* and the *London Evening News*, and also worked at Everest Books, a small publisher in London. All the while, Follett wrote fiction stories. His first books, written under the pseudonyms Symon Myles, Zachary Stone, Bernard L. Ross, and Martin Martinsen, were published but largely ignored.

It wasn't until his eleventh book, the spy thriller *Eye of the Needle* (1978; film, 1981), published under his given name, that Follett achieved his first measure of success as a novelist. The book, which features a female protagonist, sold ten million copies and earned Follett the Edgar Award for Mystery Writers of America. Subsequent novels in the genre written by Follett were also successful, including *Triple* (1979), *The Man From St. Petersburg* (1982), and *Lie Down With Lions* (1986; television miniseries, 1994).

The late 1980s marked a momentary change in direction for Follett when he wrote *The Pillars of the Earth* (1989), a work of historical fiction about the building of cathedrals in the Middle Ages; it remained on the *New York Times* best-seller list for eighteen weeks. Remarkably, it returned to the list, this time at No. 1, in 2007, thanks to its endorsement by Oprah Winfrey's book club.

Honors bestowed upon Follett include fellowships in the Welsh Academy and the Royal Society of Arts, and an honorary doctorate from the Universities of Glamorgan, Exeter, and Michigan, the latter of which holds the Ken Follett Archive. He was chair of the National Year of Reading, a London literacy initiative, in 1988-9, and president of Dyslexia Action, a charitable organization, for ten years.

Beginning in 2012, Follett published the first two books (*Fall of Giants* and *Winter of the World*) in what is known as his *Century* trilogy. The series explores the history of the twentieth century from the perspectives of five fictional families from around the globe.

FREDERICK FORSYTH

(b. 1938–)

British author Frederick Forsythe is known for his best-selling thriller novels and their journalistic style and fast-paced plots based on international political affairs and personalities.

Forsyth was born on Aug. 25, 1938, in Ashford, Kent, England. He attended the

University of Granada, Spain, and served in the Royal Air Force before becoming a journalist. He was a reporter for the British newspaper the *Eastern Daily Press* from 1958 to 1961 and a European correspondent for the Reuters news agency from 1961 to 1965. He worked as a correspondent for the British Broadcasting Corportation until he was reassigned in 1968 after criticizing British aid to Nigeria during the Biafran war; *The Biafra Story* (1969) is his nonfiction history of the war. His experiences as a news correspondent gave Forsyth the knowledge to write realistic thrillers.

Forsyth's first and most admired novel, *The Day of the Jackal* (1971; film, 1973; film *The Jackal*, 1997), is based on rumors he had heard of an actual attempt to assassinate French president Charles de Gaulle. Several other carefully researched thrillers followed, including *The Odessa File* (1972; film, 1974), about a search for a Nazi war criminal, and *The Dogs of War* (1974; film, 1980), about an uprising in a fictional African nation. Forsyth's works emphasize the power of individuals to change the world and history. Other of his novels include *The Devil's Alternative* (1979), *The Fourth Protocol* (1984; film, 1987), *The*

Negotiator (1989), *The Fist of God* (1994), *Icon* (1996), *Avenger* (2003), and *The Cobra* (2010). He also published the short-story collections *No Comebacks* (1982) and *The Veteran* (2001).

DICK FRANCIS

(b. 1920–d. 2010)

The subject of British writer Dick Francis's mystery novels came naturally to the author. A former jockey, Francis created realistic plots centered on the sport of horse racing.

Richard Stanley Francis was born in Tenby, Wales, on Oct. 31, 1920. The son of a jockey, he took up steeplechase riding in 1946, turning professional in 1948. In 1957 he had an accident that cut short his riding career. That same year he published *The Sport of Queens: The Autobiography of Dick Francis*, and until 1973 he was a racing correspondent for London's *Sunday Express*.

In 1962 Francis turned to fiction with a successful first novel, *Dead Cert* (film, 1974). Thereafter he averaged a book a year, all set in the world of horse racing.

Author Dick Francis turned his work as a jockey into fodder for several mystery novels set in the world of thoroughbreds and race tracks. © AP Images

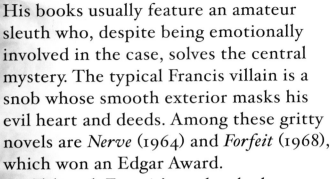

His books usually feature an amateur sleuth who, despite being emotionally involved in the case, solves the central mystery. The typical Francis villain is a snob whose smooth exterior masks his evil heart and deeds. Among these gritty novels are *Nerve* (1964) and *Forfeit* (1968), which won an Edgar Award.

Although Francis's readers had come to expect a certain amount of brutality in his work, by the 1980s he had begun to write more introspective novels. Beginning with *Reflex* (1980), the story of a mediocre jockey facing the end of his career, Francis began to examine his protagonists' inner torments. Critics welcomed this change in style. *Hot Money* (1987) is considered one of his best works.

Later novels include *Comeback* (1991), *Decider* (1993), *Come to Grief* (1995), *To the Hilt* (1996), *10 Lb. Penalty* (1997), *Second Wind* (1999), *Shattered* (2000), and *Under Orders* (2006). Late in life Francis began coauthoring novels with his son Felix, including *Dead Heat* (2007), *Silks* (2008), and *Even Money* (2009). Dick Francis died on the island of Grand Cayman on Feb. 14, 2010.

ERLE STANLEY GARDNER

(b. 1889–d. 1970)

U.S. author and lawyer Erle Stanley Gardner wrote nearly 100 detective and mystery novels that sold more than 1 million copies each, making him easily the best-selling American writer of his time. His best-known works center on the lawyer-detective Perry Mason.

Erle Stanley Gardner was born on July 17, 1889, in Malden, Mass. The son of a mining engineer, Gardner traveled extensively with his family throughout childhood. He dropped out of Valparaiso University in Valparaiso, Ind., after a brief time and settled in California, where he worked as a typist in a law firm. After three years he was admitted to the California bar (1911) and began defending poor Chinese and Mexicans as well as other clients. His interest in the friendless and unjustly accused was lifelong and led to his founding of the Court of Last Resort in the 1940s, an organization dedicated to helping men imprisoned unjustly.

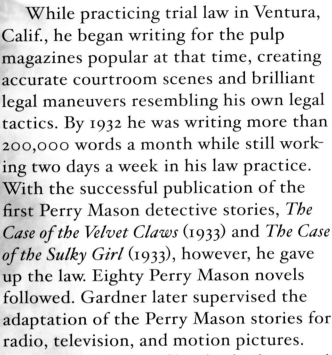

While practicing trial law in Ventura, Calif., he began writing for the pulp magazines popular at that time, creating accurate courtroom scenes and brilliant legal maneuvers resembling his own legal tactics. By 1932 he was writing more than 200,000 words a month while still working two days a week in his law practice. With the successful publication of the first Perry Mason detective stories, *The Case of the Velvet Claws* (1933) and *The Case of the Sulky Girl* (1933), however, he gave up the law. Eighty Perry Mason novels followed. Gardner later supervised the adaptation of the Perry Mason stories for radio, television, and motion pictures.

A second series of books, built around Doug Selby, a virtuous crusading district attorney, all had titles beginning "The D.A. ...": *The D.A. Calls It Murder* (1937) and *The D.A. Goes to Trial* (1940), for example. A third series, written under the pseudonym A.A. Fair, dealt with the adventures of the fat, middle-aged, greedy private detective Bertha Cool and the knowledgeable legalist Donald Lam. Gardner died on March 11, 1970, in Temecula, Calif.

The mastermind behind the Perry Mason mysteries, Erle Stanley Garner. Ray Fisher/Time & Life Pictures/Getty Images

SUE GRAFTON

(b. 1940–)

A prolific mystery author, Sue Grafton's best-selling mysteries have been published in 28 countries and translated into 26 languages. She is the author of the "alphabet series" featuring protagonist Kinsey Millhone.

Sue Taylor Grafton was born on April 24, 1940, in Louisville, K.Y. Her childhood was less than idyllic; her lawyer father and schoolteacher mother were alcoholics, a situation that led her to become essentially self-sufficient at an early age. She attended both the University of Kentucky and Western Kentucky State Teachers College, graduating from the former in 1961 with a bachelor's degree in English.

Grafton published two novels in the 1960s, *Kezjah Dane* (1967) and *The Lolly Madonna War* (1969; film, 1973), neither of which was a mystery story. Publication of the books led Grafton to a career in television writing in the 1970s. Her work in TV included the series *Rhoda* and two

Agatha Christie movies, *Sparkling Cyanide* and *Caribbean Mystery*.

Grafton's fiction-writing career took off with the publication of *A Is for Alibi* (1982), the first of the Kinsey Millhone alphabet books By 2013, Grafton had written through to *W Is for Wasted* in the series.

Readers have often wondered if Kinsey is actually the literary alter-ego of Grafton herself. Of her heroine, Grafton has said, "She is the person I might have been had I not married young and had kids. She is my unlived life." The author further fueled speculation when she published *Kinsey and Me* (2013), a collection of short stories featuring the character Kinsey accompanied by brief autobiographical sketches that illustrate the parallels between their lives.

JOHN GRISHAM

(b. 1955–)

With an ear for dialogue and an ability to make legalese understandable to the ordinary reader, lawyer John Grisham became a best-selling writer of legal thrillers.

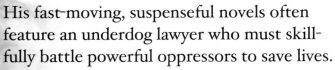

His fast-moving, suspenseful novels often feature an underdog lawyer who must skill-fully battle powerful oppressors to save lives.

Grisham was born on Feb. 8, 1955, in Jonesboro, Ark. His family moved often throughout his youth because of his father's construction jobs, but they eventually settled in Southaven, Miss., in the late 1960s. Grisham earned a bachelor's degree in accounting from Mississippi State University in 1977 and a law degree from the University of Mississippi in 1981. He returned to Southaven to set up a practice, first concentrating on criminal law and then on civil cases. In 1983, he was elected to the Mississippi House of Representatives as a Democrat and served until 1990.

Grisham began writing his first novel after observing a rape trial involving a 10-year-old victim. Stirred by the intense emotions in the courtroom, he wondered what a jury would do if the girl's father killed the attacker. Although he was already devoting more than 70 hours a week to his practice, Grisham got up early each day for three years to write what became *A Time to Kill*. Some two dozen publishers rejected the book before Wynwood Press bought the manuscript for 15,000 dollars and printed 5,000 copies in 1989.

A New York movie scout saw the manuscript for Grisham's next novel before it was sold, and Paramount studios bought the rights to it for 600,000 dollars. This brought attention from many large book publishers, and Grisham quit his practice after signing a contract with the publisher Doubleday. *The Firm* (1991) spent almost a year on the *New York Times* best-seller list and was translated into more than 25 languages. Tom Cruise starred in the movie version, which was one of the top-grossing films of 1993.

Grisham solidified his reputation as one of the most popular writers of the 1990s with *The Pelican Brief'* (1992), *The Client* (1993), *The Chamber* (1994), *The Rainmaker* (1995), *The Runaway Jury* (1996), and *The Partner* (1997). The reissue of *A Time to Kill* also did well. Other legal thrillers penned by Grisham include *The Brethren* (2000), *The Last Juror* (2004), *The Appeal* (2008), *The Associate* (2009), *The Litigators* (2011), and *The Racketeers* (2012). Film rights to Grisham's novels, among

Author John Grisham, at a 2009 book signing promoting The Associate, *in New York City.* Bryan Bedder/ Getty Images

them *The Pelican Brief* (film, 1993) and *The Client* (filmed the following year), have commanded millions of dollars.

In 2001 Grisham detoured from his formulaic legal thrillers with *A Painted House* (made-for-TV film, 2003), the story of a farm boy from rural Arkansas who discovers a troubling secret in his small town. Other nonlegal novels followed, including *Skipping Christmas* (2001; film, 2004 as *Christmas with the Kranks*), *Bleachers* (2003), *Playing for Pizza* (2007), and *Calico Joe* (2012). In 2009 he published the short-story collection *Ford County*. The following year saw *Theodore Boone: Kid Lawyer*, the first installment in a series of young-adult novels.

DASHIELL HAMMETT

(b. 1894–d. 1961)

One of Humphrey Bogart's most memorable roles was as private detective Sam Spade in the film version of *The Maltese Falcon*. The movie was based

on the novel by mystery writer Dashiell Hammett. He created the hard-boiled school of detective fiction, a tradition that was later taken up by Mickey Spillane, Ross Macdonald, and others.

Samuel Dashiell Hammett was born on May 27, 1894, in St. Mary's County, Md. At 14 he left school to work at odd jobs for eight years before joining the Pinkerton Detective Agency. He served in World War I, where he contracted tuberculosis, and spent several years afterward in army hospitals. He also served in World War II as an enlisted man.

Hammett began to publish short stories in about 1923 in pulp magazines. His first novels were *Red Harvest* and *The Dain Curse*, both published in 1929. *The Maltese Falcon* came out in 1930 and *The Glass Key* in 1931. In *The Thin Man* (1932), his last book, he created the characters Nick and Nora Charles, a detective couple about whom several movies and a television series were made. Nora was based on his friend, playwright Lillian Hellman.

Although all of his published works were written within a ten-year period, Hammett probably had more influence on the detective story than any other American author after Edgar Allan Poe. His books were the first and best attempt to render realistically the world of American crime. Hammett died in New York City on Jan. 10, 1961.

JOSEPH HANSEN

(b. 1923–d. 2004)

American writer Joseph Hansen was a published poet and novelist. He is best known as the author of a series of crime novels featuring the homosexual insurance investigator and detective Dave Brandstetter.

Hansen, who also wrote under the

American mystery writer Dashiell Hammett. Culver Pictures, Inc.

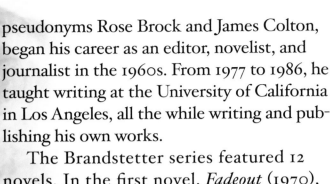

pseudonyms Rose Brock and James Colton, began his career as an editor, novelist, and journalist in the 1960s. From 1977 to 1986, he taught writing at the University of California in Los Angeles, all the while writing and publishing his own works.

The Brandstetter series featured 12 novels. In the first novel, *Fadeout* (1970), the investigator turned detective falls in love with a man whom he clears of murder charges. *Death Claims* (1973) explores surviving the death of a lover. Brandstetter investigates the murder of the owner of a bar for homosexuals in *Troublemaker* (1975). In *Early Graves* (1987) he comes out of retirement to trace a serial killer who murders men who have AIDS. The series concluded with *A Country of Old Men* (1991). The Brandstetter character also appears in several other novels and in *Brandstetter and Others* (1984), a collection of short stories.

In addition to the Brandstetter series, Hansen wrote the novels *A Smile in His Lifetime* (1981), *Backtrack* (1982), *Job's Year* (1983), and *Jack of Hearts* (1995), as well as the short-story collections *The Dog and Other Stories* (1979), *Bohannon's Book* (1988), and *Bohannon's Country* (1993). Hansen died on Nov. 24, 2004, in Laguna Beach, Calif.

PATRICIA HIGHSMITH

(b. 1921–d. 1995)

U.S. mystery writer Patricia Highsmith is known for her psychological thrillers in which characters' lives intermingle with deadly results. She is recognized primarily for the novels *Strangers on a Train* and *The Talented Mr. Ripley*, both of which were adapted into successful motion pictures.

Highsmith was born Mary Patricia Plangman on Jan. 19, 1921, in Fort Worth, Tex. Her parents separated before she was born, and she acquired the surname Highsmith from her stepfather. Her birth parents worked as commercial artists, and she found herself drawn to painting and sculpting before deciding to pursue literature. She graduated from Barnard College in New York City in 1942 and traveled to

Europe in 1949, eventually settling there. One of her early jobs as a writer was to provide plots for comic books.

In 1950 Highsmith published *Strangers on a Train*, an intriguing story of two men, one ostensibly good and the other ostensibly evil, whose lives become inextricably entangled. The following year the novel was made into

Novelist Patricia Highsmith, posing at her home in Switzerland in 1987. Ulf Andersen/Getty Images

a movie by Alfred Hitchcock. *The Talented Mr. Ripley* (1955) is the first of several books featuring the adventures of a charming murderer, Tom Ripley, who takes on the identities of his victims. The novel, which won several awards for mystery writing, was adapted for film in 1960 by René Clément as *Plein soleil* (*Purple Noon*) and again in 1999 by Anthony Minghella under its original title. Ripley also appears in *Ripley Under Ground* (1970), *Ripley's Game* (1974), *The Boy Who Followed Ripley* (1980), and *Ripley Under Water* (1991).

Among Highsmith's other books are *The Price of Salt* (1952; written under the pseudonym Claire Morgan), a tale of a love affair between a married woman and a younger, unmarried woman, and *The Animal-Lover's Book of Beastly Murder* (1975), about the killing of humans by animals. Her collections of short stories include *The Black House* (1981) and *Tales of Natural and Unnatural Catastrophes* (1987).

Highsmith also wrote on the craft of writing. In her *Plotting and Writing Suspense Fiction* (1966; revised and enlarged 1981), she held that "art has nothing to do with morality, convention, or moralizing." She died on Feb. 4, 1995, in Locarno, Switzerland.

TONY HILLERMAN

(b. 1925–d. 2008)

M ystery writer Tony Hillerman produced taut mysteries that brought
to light rich American Indian customs and
culture. His lyrical novels were prized for
their authenticity, explored the conflicts
between traditional Native American values
and those of modern society. The works
were set in the sprawling U.S. Southwest
(Arizona, Utah, Colorado, and New Mexico)
and focused on the motivation of the
suspect.

Anthony Grove Hillerman was born
in Sacred Heart, Okla. on May 27, 1925.
A natural storyteller, Hillerman spent
his youth in Depression-era Oklahoma,
where he attended a grammar school
for Indian girls and a high school with
the Potawatomie. After service in World
War II, he graduated (1946) with a B.A.
in journalism from the University of
Oklahoma.

Armed with his intimate knowledge
of and feeling of kinship with American
Indians, he began writing fiction while

serving (1965–85) as a professor (emeritus from 1985) at the University of New Mexico. His debut novel, *The Blessing Way* (1970) featured Navajo tribal officer Lieut. Joe Leaphorn, who used the latest police crime-solving methods coupled with traditional Navajo beliefs (*hozro*, or harmony) in his detection. Similar themes ran through *People of Darkness* (1980), which introduced Sgt. Jim Chee. Hillerman found commercial success in 1986 with *Skinwalkers*, the book that brought together the cynical Leaphorn, who understood but did not embrace Navajo practices, and the younger Chee, who was studying to become a Navajo *hataali*, or shaman.

Hillerman produced 18 novels in the series, ending with *The Shape Shifter* (2006), and a number of nonfiction works, including *New Mexico, Rio Grande, and Other Essays* (1992). Among his numerous awards were two from the Mystery Writers of America: the Edgar Allan Poe Award (1974, for *Dance Hall of the Dead* [1973]) and the Grand Master Award (1991). He died on Oct. 26, 2008, in Alburquerque, N.M.

SHIRLEY JACKSON

(b. 1919–d. 1965)

The works of U.S. novelist and short-story writer Shirley Jackson are often macabre explorations of the chaos and evil that lurk just beneath the surface of ordinary, everyday life. Jackson is best known for her story "The Lottery."

Shirley Hardie Jackson was born on Dec. 14, 1919, in San Francisco, Calif. She graduated from Syracuse University in 1940 and married the U.S. literary critic Stanley Edgar Hyman. They settled in North Bennington, Vt., in 1945. *Life Among the Savages* (1953) and *Raising Demons* (1957) are witty and humorous fictionalized memoirs about their life with their four children.

The light, comic tone of those books contrasted sharply with the dark pessimism of Jackson's other works. "The Lottery" (1948), a chilling tale whose meaning has been much debated, provoked widespread public outrage when it was first published in the *New Yorker*. Jackson's six finished novels, especially

The Haunting of Hill House (1959) and *We Have Always Lived in the Castle* (1962), further established her reputation as a master of Gothic horror and psychological suspense. She died on Aug. 8, 1965, in North Bennington.

STEPHEN KING

(b. 1947–)

When U.S. novelist and short-story writer Stephen King published *Carrie* in 1974, the novel became an instant success and helped to establish King's reputation as a master of horror literature. *Carrie* was quickly followed by other horror stories, with many being made into highly successful motion pictures.

Stephen Edwin King was born in Portland, Me., on Sept. 21, 1947. He began writing at an early age, and his imagination was spurred by listening to tales of horror on the radio, watching them in the movies, or reading them in paperbacks. He attended the University of Maine,

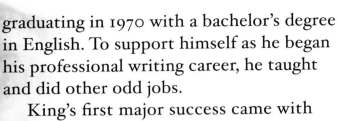

graduating in 1970 with a bachelor's degree in English. To support himself as he began his professional writing career, he taught and did other odd jobs.

King's first major success came with *Carrie* (1974; film, 1976), a story about a young girl who uses her power to move objects by telekinesis in order to wreak revenge on her tormentors. This was the first of many novels in which King blended horror, the macabre, fantasy, and science fiction. Among his works were *Salem's Lot* (1975), *The Shining* (1977; film, 1980), *The Stand* (1978), *The Dead Zone* (1979; film, 1983), *Firestarter* (1980; film, 1984), *Cujo* (1981; film, 1983), *The Running Man* (1982; film, 1987), *Christine* (1983; film, 1983), *Thinner* (1984; film, 1996), *It* (1986), *Misery* (1987; film, 1990), *The Tommyknockers* (1987), *The Dark Half* (1989; film, 1993), *Needful Things* (1991; film 1993), *Gerald's Game* (1992), *Dolores Claiborne* (1993; film, 1995), *Insomnia* (1994), *The Girl Who Loved Tom Gordon* (2000), *Dreamcatcher* (2001; film, 2003), *Cell* (2006), *Duma Key* (2008), and *Under the Dome* (2009; television mini-series, 2013). Several of these books appeared under the pseudonym Richard Bachmann. King was also the author of a serial novel, *The Dark Tower*, with the first installment, *The Gunslinger*, appearing in 1982; a seventh volume was published in 2004. *Joyland* and *Doctor Sleep*—the latter a sequel to *The Shining*—were published in 2013.

In his books King explored terror-producing themes, including vampires, rabid dogs, deranged killers, ghosts, biological warfare, and an evil automobile. In some of his later works (particularly *Gerald's Game* and *Dolores Claiborne*) he left the horror genre and provided sharply detailed psychological portraits of his major characters, who are up against challenging circumstances. Although some critics called his work undisciplined and inelegant, King was adept at using realistic detail and forceful plotting to engage and scare the reader.

By the early 1990s King's books had sold more than 100 million copies worldwide. He also wrote short stories collected in such volumes as *Night Shift* (1978) and *Just After Sunset* (2008). Some of his novels were adapted for the screen by well-known directors such as John

Horror-meister Stephen King talks to an unseen fan during a 2009 book signing in Atlanta, Ga. Taylor Hill/FilmMagic/Getty Images

Carpenter, Brian de Palma, and Stanley Kubrick. In 2000 King published *On Writing*, a book exploring both his own career and the craft of writing. That same year he released *The Plant* solely as an e-book distributed on the Internet. In 2009 his novella *Ur* was made available only to users of the Kindle electronic reading device. In 2013, King collaborated with singer and songwriter John Mellancamp to create the musical *Ghost Brothers of Darkland County*.

DEAN KOONTZ

(b. 1945–)

The popular American writer Dean Koontz has dabbled in a number of genres. Although he has produced romance and science fiction works, he is perhaps best known as a mystery, horror, and thriller writer.

Dean Ray Koontz was born on July 9, 1945, in Everett, Pa. His upbringing was markedly unstable. His father was an alcoholic and compulsive gambler who worked intermittently as a salesman. The family

lived in a poorly built home that did not have indoor plumbing until Koontz was 10.

Koontz won a fiction contest sponsored by *Atlantic Monthly* in his senior year at Shippensburg State College (now Shippensburg University). After graduation, he married his high-school sweetheart and spent one year working as a counselor for impoverished youths, followed by two years as a suburban English teacher. His wife agreed to support him for five years while he wrote full-time. It took fifteen years for Koontz to be able to support them, while his wife handled the business end of his career.

Koontz wrote under no less than 10 pseudonyms during the early part of his career, largely to avoid confusing readers when switching genres. He considers his first serious work to be 1972's *Chase*, although his first novel, *Starquest*, had been published four years earlier. His use of pen names ended with the publication of his first *New York Times* hardcover bestseller, *Strangers* (1986). Henceforth, he would write as Dean Koontz only.

Many of Koontz's other works have topped the best-seller list, including *Midnight*

(1989) and *Dragon Tears* (1993), *Watchers* (2008), and several books in the Odd Thomas series, which made their debut in 2004. In addition to novels, Koontz also has penned graphic novels (*Fear Nothing* [2010], *House of Odd* [2012]), and the children's books *I, Trixie, Who is Dog* (2009) and *Trixie and Jinx* (2010). The latter two have been adapted into computer apps. A number of movies have been made that were based on Koontz's work, from the theatrical release of *The Demon Seed* (1973; film, 1977) through several television movies, to *Odd Thomas*, based on Koontz's series of the same name, scheduled as a summer 2013 theatrical film.

JOHN LE CARRÉ

(b. 1931–)

One of the most adept and popular authors of spy fiction writes under the name John le Carré. The realism of his novels derives in great part from the knowledge of international espionage he gained while a member of the British foreign service from 1960 to 1964.

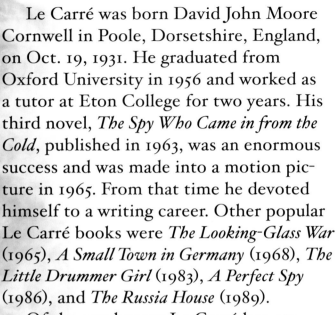

Le Carré was born David John Moore Cornwell in Poole, Dorsetshire, England, on Oct. 19, 1931. He graduated from Oxford University in 1956 and worked as a tutor at Eton College for two years. His third novel, *The Spy Who Came in from the Cold*, published in 1963, was an enormous success and was made into a motion picture in 1965. From that time he devoted himself to a writing career. Other popular Le Carré books were *The Looking-Glass War* (1965), *A Small Town in Germany* (1968), *The Little Drummer Girl* (1983), *A Perfect Spy* (1986), and *The Russia House* (1989).

Of the spy-heroes Le Carré has created, none has become more popular than the intrepid, brilliant, and sometimes plodding George Smiley, an agent for the British Secret Intelligence Service, MI-6. He is the main character in Le Carré's first two novels, *Call for the Dead* (1961) and *A Murder of Quality* (1962), as well as in the three later novels *Tinker, Tailor, Soldier, Spy* (1974; film, 2011), *The Honourable Schoolboy* (1977), and *Smiley's People* (1980). The last three are known collectively as the Karla trilogy, named after Smiley's Russian nemesis in the three books.

Author of several best-selling spy thrillers John Le Carré.
Dave Hogan/Getty Images

SHERIDAN LE FANU

(b. 1814–d. 1873)

Sheridan Le Fanu was an Irish writer of ghost stories and mystery novels. He was celebrated for his ability to evoke the ominous atmosphere of a haunted house.

Joseph Sheridan Le Fanu was born in Dublin on Aug. 28. 1814. He belonged to an old Dublin Huguenot family and was related on his mother's side to poet and playwright Richard Brinsley Sheridan. Educated at Trinity College, Dublin, Le Fanu became a lawyer in 1839 but soon abandoned law for journalism.

The Purcell Papers, written while he was a student, were collected in three volumes in 1880. Between 1845 and 1873 he published 14 novels, of which *Uncle Silas* (1864) and *The House by the Churchyard* (1863) are the best known. He also contributed numerous short stories, mostly of ghosts and the supernatural, to the *Dublin University Magazine*, which he owned and edited from 1861 to 1869.

In a *Glass Darkly* (1872), a book of five long stories, is generally regarded as his best work. Included in the collection is his classic story "Carmilla," which popularized the theme of the female vampire. Le Fanu also owned the *Dublin Evening Mail* and other newspapers. He died on Feb. 7, 1873, in Dublin.

ELMORE LEONARD

(b. 1925–d. 2013)

Although Elmore (Dutch) Leonard's crime fiction was often called "hardboiled," it bore little resemblance to most other detective novels. Leonard rarely used the same character in more than one book, and his protagonists were frequently "good guys" only in the sense that they were somewhat more ethical than their enemies. He never planned his complicated plots in advance, preferring to watch them grow out of his characters. That, combined with his uncanny ear for dialogue, his effective use of sometimes grisly violence, and his unforced use of satiric wit and ironic plot twists, gave his books a natural sense of reality.

Elmore John Leonard, Jr., was born in New Orleans, Louisiana, on October 11, 1925. His father, who worked for General

Motors, moved the family repeatedly until they settled in 1935 near Detroit, Mich., where Leonard remained. An avid athlete in high school, he was nick-named for Dutch Leonard, a pitcher for the Washington Senators. Leonard served in the United States Navy during World War II, received a doctorate from the University of Detroit in 1950, and then went to work for a Detroit adver-tising agency, where he wrote copy for Chevrolet trucks.

A fondness for Western movies led him to write Western stories in his spare time. His early fiction appeared in such publications as *Zane Grey Western, The Saturday Evening Post*, and various pulp magazines. His first novel, *The Bounty Hunters*, was published in 1953. He quit advertising after his fifth novel, *Hombre* (1961), was published, but he earned extra money writing educational films for Encyclopaedia Britannica and doing other freelance writing work.

With the success of the film version of *Hombre* (1967), Leonard was finally able to devote himself to fiction. He wrote several screenplays, for *The Moonshine War* (1970),

Novelist Elmore Leonard tried his hand at writing westerns and general fiction before turning to the crime thrillers that have made him famous. Vince Bucci/Getty Images

Joe Kidd (1972), and *Mr. Majestyk* (1974), before switching to urban crime novels in the mid-1970s. In the 1980s he shifted his locales from Detroit to the seamier side of Miami. With *Stick* and *LaBrava* (both 1983) Leonard began to gain notice. The

film version of *Stick* (1985) was a critical and box-office failure, a fact that Leonard blamed on its divergence from his original screenplay.

His successes during the 1970s and early 1980s were significant enough, however, to build a strong cult following, which erupted into widespread acclaim in 1985 with the publication of *Glitz*, a novel based mainly in Puerto Rico and Atlantic City. The book became a best-seller and received an outpouring of critical attention—including a cover story in *Newsweek*—that finally awarded the author the recognition that had eluded him for more than 30 years. His novels *Bandits* (1987), *Touch* (1988), *Freaky Deaky* (1988), *Killshot* (1989), *Get Shorty* (1990), *Maximum Bob* (1991), *Rum Punch* (1992), and *Pronto* (1993) were critical successes and national best-sellers. Leonard continued his best-seller streak into the 21st century with novels such as *The Hot Kid* (2005) and *Up in Honey's Room* (2007).

Leonard's skill in depicting the convoluted world of crime in America continued to attract the attention of filmmakers. *Get Shorty* was made into a well-received film of the same title (1995), and the screenplay for director Quentin Tarantino's movie *Jackie Brown* (1997) was based on Leonard's book *Rum Punch.* Later works *Out of Sight* (1996; film, 1998) and *Cuba Libre* (1998; film, 2005), set in Havana, reinforced Leonard's position as one of the most prolific and respected of American crime writers.

In 1983 the Mystery Writers of America gave *LaBrava* the Edgar Allan Poe Award. *Maximum Bob* won the first annual International Association of Crime Writers' award for the best crime book of the year in 1991. In 1992 the Mystery Writers of America presented Leonard with the Grand Master Award, in recognition of his pre-eminence in the field of mystery writing. Leonard died at home in Bloomfield Village, Mich., on Aug. 20, 2013.

H.P. LOVECRAFT

(b. 1890–d. 1937)

American H.P. Lovecraft was a noted author of fantastic and macabre short novels and stories. He is considered one of

the 20th-century masters of the Gothic tale of terror.

Howard Phillips Lovecraft was born in Providence, R.I., on Aug. 20, 1890. He was interested in science from childhood. Though lifelong poor health prevented him from attending college, he was able to make a living as a ghostwriter and rewrite man, which is a newspaper reporter who works in an office, writing articles based on reports submitted by others.

From 1923 on, most of Lovecraft's short stories appeared in the magazine *Weird Tales*. His Cthulhu Mythos series of tales describe ordinary New Englanders' encounters with horrific beings of extraterrestrial origin. In these short stories, Lovecraft's intimate knowledge of New England's geography and culture is blended with an elaborate original mythology. His other short stories deal with similarly terrifying phenomena in which horror and morbid fantasy acquire an unexpected verisimilitude. *The Case of Charles Dexter Ward* (1927; published posthumously 1941), *At the Mountains of Madness* (1931, published 1936), and *The Shadow over Innsmouth* (1931, published 1936) are considered his best short novels.

Lovecraft spent most of his life in seclusion and poverty. His fame as a writer increased after his death on March 15, 1937, in Providence.

ROBERT LUDLUM

(b. 1927–d. 2001)

R obert Ludlum was a best-selling author of suspense novels. His books sold more than 220 million copies in some 40 countries.

Ludlum was born in New York City on May 25, 1927. He worked as an actor and theatrical producer for 20 years, and did not write his first novel until he was in his 40s. That first book, *The Scarlatti Inheritance* (1971), was an instant commercial hit.

Ludlum was perhaps best known for his trilogy of novels starring the amnesiac assassin Jason Bourne. All three—*The Bourne Identity* (1980), *The Bourne Supremacy* (1986), and *The Bourne Ultimatum* (1990)—were made into popular movies starring Matt Damon, in 2002, 2004, and 2007, respectively.

Other successful thrillers penned by him include *The Osterman Weekend* (1972), *The Icarus Agenda* (1988), and *The Prometheus Deception* (2000). He also wrote numerous books under the pseudonyms Jonathan Ryder (including *Treyvayne* [1973]) and Michael Shepherd.

Ludlum died of a heart attack on March 12, 2001, in Naples, Fla. Novels based on material left behind by Ludlum have been published with the help of authors selected by his estate.

STEPHENIE MEYER

(b. 1973–)

U.S. author Stephenie Meyer is known for her series of vampire-themed novels. The popular series, blending vivid characterizations, obsessive love, and teen angst, was a hit among teenage girls.

Born Stephenie Morgan on Dec. 24, 1973, in Hartford, Conn., she was raised in Phoenix, Ariz. She received a National Merit Scholarship and attended Brigham Young University, where she graduated in

The enormous success of her series of vampire-themed novels for young adults has thrust author Stephenie Meyer into the limelight, beginning with the 2005 publication of her first book, Twilight.
Karen Shell

109

1997 with a bachelor's degree in English literature. She married in 1994 and was a stay-at-home mother to her three sons.

Meyer began writing her first book, *Twilight* (2005; film, 2008), after she had a dream about the subject. The book introduces readers to teenager Bella Swan and her vampire boyfriend, Edward Cullen. Meyer portrayed Edward as a sensitive and thoughtful figure, rather than a bloodsucking creature of the night. In Meyer's depiction, some vampires, like Edward and his family, do not drink human blood. They also do not turn into bats or sleep in coffins, and they travel abroad in daylight. Meyer completed the book in three months.

Twilight won many accolades, and *Publishers Weekly* named Meyer one of the most promising new authors of 2005. The publisher Little, Brown and Co. offered her a lucrative book deal. Subsequent novels in *The Twilight Saga*, as Meyer's series of four books came to be known, were *New Moon* (2006; film, 2009), *Eclipse* (2007; film, 2010), and *Breaking Dawn* (2008; film, in two parts, 2011 and 2012).

Meyer is also the author of *The Host* (2008; film, 2013), which featured a similar focus on romantic entanglements between young adults and paranormal beings, this time centering on extraterrestrials as the alien element. The novel extended Meyer's commercial success. In 2010 Meyer published *The Short Second Life of Bree Tanner*, a novella about a "newborn" vampire that appeared in *Eclipse*.

WALTER MOSLEY

(b. 1952–)

Walter Mosley is an American author of mystery stories noted for their realistic portrayals of segregated inner-city life. He is perhaps best known for his series featuring the protagonist Easy Rawlins.

Mosley was born on Jan. 12, 1952, in Los Angeles, Calif. He attended Goddard College and Johnson State College, and he became a computer programmer before publishing his first novel, *Devil in a Blue Dress* (1990; film, 1995). Set in 1948, the novel introduces Ezekiel ("Easy") Rawlins, an unwilling amateur detective from the

Watts section of Los Angeles. It presents period issues of race relations and mores as the unemployed Rawlins is hired to find a white woman who frequents jazz clubs in black districts.

In all his Easy Rawlins novels, Mosley used period detail and slang to create authentic settings and characters, especially the earnest, complex main character, who continually is faced with personal, social, and moral dilemmas. In *A Red Death* (1991), set during the McCarthy era of the 1950s, Rawlins is blackmailed by the FBI into spying on a labor union organizer. In *White Butterfly* (1992) the police call on Rawlins to help investigate the vicious murders of four young women—three black and one white. Other novels featuring Rawlins include *Black Betty* (1994) and *A Little Yellow Dog* (1996). For the publication of *Gone Fishin'* (1997), a prequel to *Devil in a Blue Dress*, Mosley chose a small independent black publisher, Black Classic Press, over his longtime publisher W.W. Norton. The series continued with *Bad Boy Brawly Brown* (2002), *Little Scarlet* (2004), *Cinnamon Kiss* (2005), *Blonde Faith* (2007), and *Little Green* (2013). A collection of short stories featuring Easy Rawlins, *Six Easy Pieces*, was published by Washington Square Press in 2003.

Mosley revisited the setting of Los Angeles in the 1950s with the publication of *Fearless Jones* (2001), introducing the title character and bookseller Paris Minton, and its sequel, *Fear Itself* (2003). Mosley's other novels include *RL's Dream* (1995), *The Man in My Basement* (2004), and *Diablerie* (2008). *Always Outnumbered, Always Outgunned* (1997; filmed as *Always Outnumbered* for television, 1998), a collection of stories set in contemporary Watts, features the ex-convict Socrates Fortlow. Mosley returned to the Fortlow character in the stories of *Walkin' the Dog* (1999). *The Tempest Tales*, which centers on a dead man whose refusal to accept St. Peter's judgment results in him being returned to earth, was adapted into his first play, *The Fall of Heaven*, which was staged in 2010.

Mosley also tried his hand at other genres. He ventured into science fiction in *Blue Light* (1998) and *Futureland* (2001), a group of interlocking stories, as well as nonfiction in *Workin' on the Chain Gang: Shaking Off the Dead Hand of History* (2000) and *What Next: A Memoir Toward World Peace* (2003).

E. PHILLIPS OPPENHEIM

(b. 1866–d. 1946)

The internationally popular English author E. Phillips Oppenheim wrote of international espionage and intrigue. His novels, volumes of short stories, and plays, totaling more than 150, are peopled with sophisticated heroes, adventurous spies, and dashing noblemen.

Edward Phillips Oppenheim was born in London, England, on Oct. 22, 1866. After leaving school at age 17 to help in his father's leather business, he wrote in his spare time. His first novel, *Expiation* (1886), and subsequent thrillers won him the attention of a wealthy New York businessman who bought out the leather business and made Oppenheim a high-salaried director, freeing him to devote most of his time to writing.

Among Oppenheim's best-known works are *The Long Arm of Mannister* (1910), *The Moving Finger* (1911), and *The Great Impersonation* (1920). He died on Feb. 3, 1946, in St. Peter Port, Guernsey, in the Channel Islands.

British author E. Phillips Oppenheim, whose works were full of intrigue and derring-do. George Grantham Bain Collection/ Library of Congress, Washington, D.C. (Digital File Number: LC-DIG-ggbain-00608)

SARA PARETSKY

(b. 1947–)

American mystery writer Sara Paretsky is credited with breaking the gender barrier in detective fiction with her popular series of novels featuring V.I. Warshawski, a female private investigator. Her books are set in and around Chicago.

Paretsky was born in Ames, Iowa, on June 8, 1947. After receiving a Ph.D. in history and an M.B.A. from the University of Chicago in 1977, she worked for a large insurance company. She did not begin writing full time until 1985.

Warshawski, her wisecracking, independent, passionate, and compassionate female private detective, made her first appearance in *Indemnity Only* (1982). In other of the series's novels, such as *Deadlock* (1984) and *Killing Orders* (1985), the sleuth became the target of violence and uncovered conspiracies involving big business, organized crime, and even the Roman Catholic Church. Paretsky explored social issues in many of her books, including *Bitter Medicine* (1987),

Burn Marks (1990), *Guardian Angel* (1992), and *Tunnel Vision* (1994). Many critics considered Paretsky's best novel to be *Blood Shot* (1988), in which Warshawski discover that a chemical company is poisoning her childhood neighborhood for material gain.

Paretsky broke from her heroine with the publication of *Ghost Country* (1998), which features a pair of debutante sisters as amateur detectives. The Warshawski series picks up again with *Hard Time* (1999). Subsequent books in the series include *Total Recall* (2001), *Blacklist* (2003), *Fire Sale* (2005), *Hardball* (2009), *Body Work* (2010), *Breakdown* (2012), and *Critical Mass* (2013).

In the mid-1980s Paretsky helped found Sisters in Crime to promote the work of other women mystery writers and challenge the publication of crime stories marred by gratuitous violence against women. She edited *A Woman's Eye*, a collection of crime stories by women, in 1991. *Writing in an Age of Silence*, a memoir, was published in 2007. The next year, Paretsky published the non-Warshawski contemporary novel *Bleeding Kansas*.

ROBERT B. PARKER

(b. 1932–d. 2010)

Robert B. Parker's doctoral thesis was on the crime writers Dashiell Hammett and Raymond Chandler. He used what he learned from studying these authors and their works to create his most well-known character, a private investigator known by his surname, Spenser.

Robert Brown Parker was born on Sept. 17, 1932, in Springfield, Mass. He earned his bachelor of arts degree from Colby College in Maine, and his master's and doctoral degrees in English literature from Boston University.

Parker's thirty-seven year career as a crime novelist began with 1973's *The Godwulf Manuscript*, in which readers were first introduced to Spenser. Parker's protagonist has been described as a modern-day Philip Marlowe: tough yet sensitive, loyal, and with a playful sense of humor.

In addition to Spenser, Parker also created other series-worthy characters. Eleven novels, beginning with *Night Passage* (1997) featured Jesse Stone, a Massachusetts police chief. Six other books were centered on Sunny Randall, a female private detective in Boston.

The first book in that series was *Family Honor* (1999). He also wrote westerns, notably 2005's *Appaloosa*, and three young adult novels. Parker had the privilege of completing an unfinished novel by his idol, Raymond Chandler, titled *Poodle Springs* (1989).

Parker's novels have had great success in television and film. His Spenser character was the basis for the 1985-88 ABC series *Spenser for Hire*, starring Robert Urich. Tom Selleck has appeared as Jesse Stone in a number of made-for-TV movies, including *Jesse Stone: No Remorse* (2010) and *Jesse Stone: Benefit of the Doubt* (2012). A feature film, *Appaloosa*, based on the novel of the same name, was released in 2008. Parker died on Jan. 19, 2010, in Cambridge, Mass.

JAMES PATTERSON

(b. 1947–)

Prolific U.S. author James Patterson is principally known for his thriller and suspense novels. During the late 20th and early 21st centuries, his work consistently made the best-seller lists. In 2005 he began to write young-adult fiction.

Popular novelist James Patterson, greeting fans and signing copies of his latest work in 2009. Jason Kempin/WireImage/Getty Images

James Brendan Patterson, Jr., was born on March 22, 1947, in Newburgh, New York. He received a bachelor's degree in English from Manhattan College in 1969 and a master's degree from Vanderbilt University in 1970. Although he had originally intended to complete a doctorate, he instead quit school. His first job was as a junior copywriter at an advertising agency, J. Walter Thompson Co.,

in New York City. There he created the slo-
gan "I'm a Toys 'R' Us kid," and he eventually
became CEO (1988) and chairman (1990) of
the company's North America division.

At the same time, Patterson actively pur-
sued a literary career. His first fiction book
was a dark crime novel titled *The Thomas
Berryman Number* (1976), which won the Edgar
Allan Poe Award for best first novel from
the Mystery Writers of America. He then
wrote several similar novels, but they failed to
attract much attention from either critics or
the reading public.

By the early 1990s, Patterson had
changed his writing style, using unadorned
prose, short chapters, and fast-paced plots.
His novel *Along Came a Spider* (1993; film,
2001) was one of the first to be written in
this vein. In order to promote it, he created and financed a television commercial
for it. The book, a grisly thriller featuring African American homicide detective
Alex Cross, became an instant best seller.
Its protagonist resurfaced in more than a
dozen other sequels, including *Kiss the Girls*
(1995; film, 1997), *Mary, Mary* (2005), and
Kill Alex Cross (2011).

In 1996 Patterson quit his advertising job
to concentrate on writing. While continuing

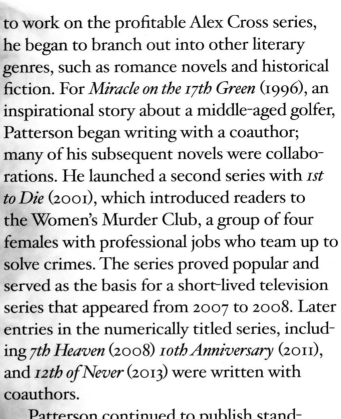

to work on the profitable Alex Cross series, he began to branch out into other literary genres, such as romance novels and historical fiction. For *Miracle on the 17th Green* (1996), an inspirational story about a middle-aged golfer, Patterson began writing with a coauthor; many of his subsequent novels were collaborations. He launched a second series with *1st to Die* (2001), which introduced readers to the Women's Murder Club, a group of four females with professional jobs who team up to solve crimes. The series proved popular and served as the basis for a short-lived television series that appeared from 2007 to 2008. Later entries in the numerically titled series, including *7th Heaven* (2008) *10th Anniversary* (2011), and *12th of Never* (2013) were written with coauthors.

Patterson continued to publish standalone novels as well. Among them were *Honeymoon* (2005), which traces the efforts of an FBI agent to track down a femme fatale, and *Sail* (2008), which centers around a family trying to evade hitmen while on a boat trip. *Sundays at Tiffany's* (2008; filmed for television 2010) was a supernatural romance written with Gabrielle Charbonnet, and *The Christmas Wedding* (2011) was a family drama written with Richard DiLallo. The nonfiction *The*

Murder of King Tut: The Plot to Kill the Child King (2009; with Martin Dugard) explores the centuries-old mystery surrounding the death of the Egyptian pharoah.

In 2005, after discovering that his son lacked an interest in reading, Patterson created the *Maximum Ride* series of science-fiction novels. Although the books were aimed at young adults, they were designed to appeal to readers of all ages. The overwhelming success of the *Maximum Ride* stories led him to develop the *Daniel X* and *Witch & Wizard* series of children's fantasy books. Eventually, all three series were adapted into graphic novels. Patterson also established the Pageturner Awards, which gave funding to educators and libraries, in 2005; however, they were discontinued three years later. In 2011 Patterson founded a Web site to promote childhood reading and to provide lists of suggested texts for different age and interest groups.

Though some critics have called Patterson's work shallow and formulaic, he is nonetheless recognized as a publishing phenomenon, capable of producing multiple best sellers each year. By the second decade of the 21st century, he had penned (alone or with a

coauthor) several dozen novels, with world-wide sales exceeding 200 million copies.

EDGAR ALLAN POE

(b. 1809–d. 1849)

The greatest American teller of mystery and suspense tales in the 19th century was Edgar Allan Poe. In his mysteries he invented the modern detective story. In Poe's poems, like his tales, his characters are tortured by nameless fears and longings. Today Poe is acclaimed as one of America's greatest writers, but in his own unhappy lifetime he knew little but failure.

Edgar Poe was born in Boston, Mass., on Jan. 19, 1809. His parents were touring actors. Orphaned at age 3, he was taken into the home of John Allan, a merchant of Richmond, Va. His wife reared Edgar as her son, but Allan accepted the boy largely to please her. Later Poe took Allan as his middle name, but his signature was usually Edgar A. Poe.

Poe moved back to Boston on his own in 1827. There he persuaded a printer to issue some of his early poems in a small pamphlet.

It was called *Tamerlane and Other Poems*, and the title page said simply "By a Bostonian."

With his money soon gone, Poe enlisted in the army under the name of Edgar A. Perry. In his two years in the army, he rose to be regimental sergeant major. Poe was granted an honorable discharge from the army. He then sought an appointment to the United States Military Academy at West Point, N.Y. He waited for more than a year. In the meantime he lived in Baltimore, Md., with his father's widowed sister, Maria Clemm, and her young daughter, Virginia. While there he published another volume of poetry, *Al Aaraaf, Tamerlane, and Minor Poems* (1829). On July 1, 1830, he was sworn in as a West Point cadet. He hated the discipline and the restraint of the school. He deliberately neglected his classes and duties and was expelled after eight months.

For the next four years Poe struggled to earn a living as a writer. He returned to Mrs. Clemm's home and submitted stories to magazines. His first success came in 1833, when he entered a short-story contest and won a prize of 50 dollars for the story "MS. Found in a Bottle." By 1835 he was the editor of the *Southern Literary Messenger*. He married

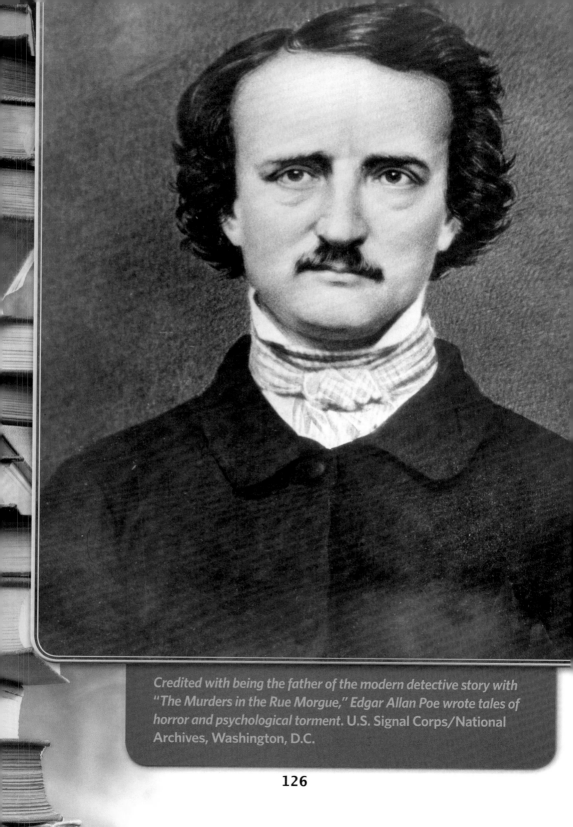

Credited with being the father of the modern detective story with "The Murders in the Rue Morgue," Edgar Allan Poe wrote tales of horror and psychological torment. U.S. Signal Corps/National Archives, Washington, D.C.

his cousin Virginia, who was only 13, and Mrs. Clemm stayed with the couple. The Poes had no children.

Poe's stories, poems, and criticism in the magazine soon attracted attention, and he looked for wider opportunities. From 1837 to 1839 he tried freelance writing in New York City and Philadelphia but earned very little. Again he tried editing (1839–42). His work was praised, but he was paid little. His efforts to organize his own magazine were unsuccessful. For the next two years he turned again to freelance writing.

Many of his best stories were written as part of his editorial work. Even those he sold for a fee rarely brought him more than 100 dollars each, but they gave him great publicity. Some of these were: "The Narrative of Arthur Gordon Pym" (1838); "The Fall of the House of Usher" (1839); *Tales of the Grotesque and Arabesque* (appeared 1839; dated 1840); "The Murders in the Rue Morgue" (1841), considered the first detective story; and "The Gold Bug" (1843). During this time his wife showed symptoms of tuberculosis.

In 1844 Poe and his family moved to New York City. There he wrote the "Balloon Hoax" for the *Sun*, and became subeditor of the *New York Mirror* under N.P. Willis. By now Poe

was well known in literary circles, and the publication of *The Raven and Other Poems* and a selection of his *Tales*, both in 1845, enhanced his reputation. That same year he became editor of the *Broadway Journal*, a short-lived weekly, in which he republished most of his short stories. The Poes lived in a cottage in Fordham (now in the borough of the Bronx). There Poe wrote for *Godey's Lady's Book* gossipy sketches about personalities of the day, which led to a libel suit. The couple was comfortable for a time, but his wife soon became sicker. Poe also grew weaker and became more dissipated. During the winter of 1846–47 they had little food or fuel. Virginia Poe died on Jan. 30, 1847.

After his wife's death Poe became increasingly depressed and erratic. He courted various women in a vain attempt to find solace for the loss of his wife. His lecture "Eureka," a transcendental explanation of the universe hailed as a masterpiece by some critics and as nonsense by others, was published in 1848. In 1849 he became engaged to a childhood sweetheart, who by then was a wealthy Richmond widow. After making wedding plans, he set out for New York City from Richmond but disappeared in Baltimore. He was found five days after he disappeared and

was very near death. He died without regaining full consciousness four days later on Oct. 7, 1849. Poe was buried in Baltimore.

Poe was the first American author to be widely read outside the United States. His reputation in France, especially, was enhanced by the French poet Charles Baudelaire, who read and translated Poe's works in the 1850s. Poe was elected to the United States Hall of Fame in 1910. Since then his reputation in literature has been secure.

ELLERY QUEEN

Manfred B. Lee (b. 1905–d. 1971)
Frederic Dannay (b. 1905–d. 1982)

The cousins Manfred B. Lee and Frederic Dannay cowrote a series of more than 35 detective novels featuring a character named Ellery Queen. They took the name of their most popular detective as a pseudonym.

Lee was born Manford Lepofsky in Brooklyn, N.Y., on Jan. 11, 1905. Dannay was born Daniel Nathan in Brooklyn on Oct. 20, 1905. They first collaborated on an impulsive entry for a detective-story contest; the success of the result, *The Roman Hat Mystery*

(1929), started Ellery Queen on his career. After the publication of two more mysteries, the cousins were able to become full-time writers. They took turns creating plots and writing stories about the sleuth Queen, whose adventures have been adapted for radio, television, and film. The pair also used the pseudonym Barnaby Ross when writing about their second detective creation, Drury Lane. They would hold debates posing as Queen and Ross, who were believed by all to be two distinct authors.

Dannay and Lee founded *Ellery Queen's Mystery Magazine* in 1941. They also edited numerous anthologies, including *101 Years' Entertainment: Great Detective Stories, 1841–1941* (1945), and cofounded Mystery Writers of America. Lee died on April 3, 1971, near Waterbury, Conn. Dannay died on Sept. 3, 1982, in White Plains, N.Y.

ANNE RICE

(b. 1941–)

American author Anne Rice is best known for her novels about vampires

and other supernatural creatures. She has also written books about angels and the life of Jesus Christ.

Born Howard Allen O'Brien on Oct. 4, 1941, in New Orleans, La., Rice hated her first name so much that she changed it to Anne in the first grade. The city of New Orleans, with its elaborate cemeteries and voodoo heritage, was an ideal place to grow up amid a family of imaginative storytelling Irish Catholics. In 1956 her mother died of alcoholism, and before long the teenage Anne disavowed her faith in God. She finished high school in Texas, attended Texas Woman's University, married poet Stan Rice when she was 20, and received a B.A. and an M.A. from San Francisco State College. Her daughter Michelle was just five years old when she died of leukemia, a loss that devastated Rice.

Rice wrote her first novel in just five weeks. *Interview with the Vampire* (1976; film, 1994) included a Michelle-like child who gains eternal life when she becomes a vampire. *Interview* was the first of Rice's best-selling *Vampire Chronicles*; other books in the series include *The Vampire Lestat* (1985), *The Queen of the Damned* (1988), *The Tale of the Body Thief* (1992), *Memnoch the Devil* (1995),

Author Anne Rice, posing with a rosey eyed skull and copies of her best-selling novels, in 1992. Bryce Lankard/Getty Images

The Vampire Armand (1998), *Merrick* (2000), *Blood and Gold* (2001), *Blackwood Farm* (2002), and *Blood Canticle* (2003). The novels focused largely on the ageless vampire Lestat and a fictitious history of vampires that begins in ancient Egypt.

Rice also wrote about real-life outsiders in two historical novels, *The Feast of All Saints* (1979) and *Cry to Heaven* (1982). Eroticism distinguished *The Sleeping Beauty Novels*, three stories (1983–85) published under the pseudonym A.N. Roquelaure that some critics classified as "pornography." She also published two novels as Anne Rampling.

In 1988 Rice moved back to New Orleans to live in a Victorian mansion that became the setting for three novels about the Mayfair witches—*The Witching Hour* (1990), *Lasher* (1993), and *Taltos* (1994). She subsequently began a second vampire series that featured *Pandora* (1998) and *Vittorio the Vampire* (1999), the latter of which Rice described as her vampire answer to Romeo and Juliet.

In the late 1990s Rice returned to her Catholic faith after spending most of her life as an atheist. Among her later works are *Christ the Lord: Out of Egypt* (2005) and *Christ the Lord: The Road to Cana* (2008). The memoir *Called Out of Darkness: A Spiritual Confession* was published in 2008. The novel *Angel Time* (2009)

was the first in what Rice projected to be a series of "metaphysical thrillers" about angels.

DOROTHY L. SAYERS

(b. 1893–d. 1957)

A British scholar and novelist, Dorothy L. Sayers wrote numerous mystery stories featuring the witty and charming detective Lord Peter Wimsey. She also published notable translations of literary classics.

The daughter of a reverend, Dorothy Leigh Sayers was born on June 13, 1893, in Oxford, Oxfordshire, England. She received a degree in medieval literature from Somerville College, University of Oxford, in 1915; she was one of the first women to graduate from the university. In London she worked as a copywriter in an advertising agency, which she later made the setting for her novel *Murder Must Advertise* (1933). In 1926 she married Arthur Fleming.

Sayers's first major published work was *Whose Body?* (1923), a fairly standard detective novel but for her creation of Lord Peter, the dashing young gentleman-scholar whose intelligence and native curiosity set him apart from the ordinary detective. The book was followed by one or two novels a year for about 15 years—including such well-known volumes as *The Unpleasantness at the Bellona Club* (1928); *Strong Poison* (1930), in which she introduced Lord Peter's future wife, Harriet Vane; *Have His Carcase* (1932); *The Nine Tailors* (1934); *Gaudy Night* (1935); and *Busman's Honeymoon* (1937). Both Lord Peter and another of Sayers's creations, Montague Egg, are featured in short stories.

With G.K. Chesterton and others, Sayers founded the Detection Club, a group composed of mystery writers, and they published a parody of the detective story in a novel entitled *The Floating Admiral* (1931). Sayers also published a three-volume anthology of detective stories entitled *Great Short Stories of Detection, Mystery and Horror* (1928, 1931, 1934; U.S. title, *The Omnibus of Crime*).

After the late 1930s Sayers wrote no more detective fiction, concentrating rather on theological dramas, radio plays,

and verse. She made several scholarly translations, including Anglo-Norman poet Thomas's *Tristan in Britanny* (1929) and *The Song of Roland* (1957). Her impressive and witty translation of Dante's *Divine Comedy*, which she published as *The Comedy of Dante Alighieri, the Florentine*, was issued in three volumes—*Hell* (1949), *Purgatory* (1955), and *Paradise* (1962). Sayers died on Dec. 17, 1957, in Witham, Essex, England.

MARY SHELLEY

(b. 1797–d. 1851)

The English Romantic writer Mary Wollstonecraft Shelley is remembered primarily for her classic Gothic novel *Frankenstein*. The book gave birth to what was to become one of the Western world's best-known monsters.

The only daughter of social philosopher William Godwin and feminist Mary Wollstonecraft, Mary Wollstonecraft Godwin was born on August 30, 1797, in London, England. She met the young poet Percy Bysshe Shelley in the spring

Portrait of Gothic novelist Mary Shelley, best known as the author of Frankenstein. Album/Prisma/SuperStock

of 1814 and eloped with him to France in July of that year. The couple were married in 1816, after Shelley's first wife had committed suicide. Mary Shelley apparently came as near as any woman could to meeting Percy Shelley's requirements for his life's partner: "one who can feel poetry and understand philosophy." After her husband's death in 1822, she returned to England and devoted herself to publicizing Shelley's writings and to educating their only surviving child, Percy Florence Shelley. She published her late husband's *Posthumous Poems* (1824) and edited his *Poetical Works* (1839), with long and invaluable notes, and his prose works. Her *Journal* and letters are a rich source of biographical information.

Mary Shelley's best-known novel is *Frankenstein, or The Modern Prometheus* (1818), in which she narrates the dreadful consequences that arise after a scientist has artificially created a human being. The novel belongs to the contemporary Gothic school, which used horror as its primary device. It offered fertile ground for such typically Romantic themes as the relationship of science to humanity and the embodied alter ego. The monster in this novel inspired a similar creature in several famous U.S. horror films of the 1930s.

Mary Shelley wrote several other novels, such as *Valperga* (1823), *The Fortunes of Perkin Warbeck* (1830), *Lodore* (1835), and *Falkner* (1837), but *The Last Man* (1826), an account of the future destruction of the human race by a plague, is still ranked as her best work. Her travel book *History of a Six Weeks' Tour* (1817) recounts the continental tour she and Shelley took in 1814 following their elopement and then describes their summer near Geneva in 1816. Mary Shelley died in London on February 1, 1851.

GEORGES SIMENON

(b. 1903–d. 1989)

The creator of the compassionate, streetwise Parisian sleuth, Inspector Jules Maigret, was Georges Simenon. A Belgian-born French writer, he was said to have published more novels than any other 20th-century author. More than

Prolific author Georges Simenon, posing with a canine friend, published detective fiction under his own name and various pseudonyms. © Jerry Bauer

400 of these—short and sparely written—came out under his own name.

Georges Joseph Christian Simenon was born in Liège, Belgium, on Feb. 13, 1903. He left school at age 16 and worked at odd jobs before trying to become a professional writer. In 1921 he became a night police reporter for a Liège newspaper and soon thereafter published his first novel using the abbreviated name Georges Sim.

In 1922, after army service, Simenon moved to Paris and began writing pulp novels in his spare time. Because of his instant popularity, much of his work was translated into at least 50 languages. His autobiography, *Intimate Memoirs* (1981), was published in English in 1984. From 1945 to 1955 the writer lived in the United States before returning to France and finally making his home in Switzerland.

The unassuming Inspector Maigret, one of the best-known characters in detective fiction, was introduced in *The Strange Case of Peter the Lett*, published in 1931. Before Simenon abandoned Maigret for psychological novels two years later, he dashed off 19 books in the series. He returned to the character in 1940 and wrote another 65 Maigret mysteries.

141

Georges Simenon died in Lausanne, Switzerland on Sept. 4, 1989.

MAJ SJÖWALL AND PER WAHLÖÖ

Maj Sjöwall (b. 1935–)
Per Wahlöö (b. 1926–d. 1975)

The Swedish husband-and-wife team of Per Wahlöö and Maj Sjöwall were journalists and innovative writers of detective fiction. They used the popular form of the detective story as a vehicle for social criticism.

Per Wahlöö was born on Aug. 5, 1926, in Göteborg, Sweden, and Maj Sjöwall was born on Sept. 25, 1935, in Stockholm. They married in 1962. Together they wrote a series of detective stories in which Martin Beck and his colleagues at the Central Bureau of Investigation in Stockholm were the main characters.

From *Roseanna*, published in 1965, to *The Terrorists*, published in 1975, the series consists of ten novels in which the crime itself is subordinate to social commentary. Both the police force and the criminals mirror the shifting social forces within the Swedish welfare state. The authors strongly criticize abuses of power and the systematic use of propaganda in society. Many of these same motifs appear in Wahlöö's novels of the late 1950s and early 1960s. Wahlöö died on June 22, 1975, in Malmö, Sweden.

ALEXANDER MCCALL SMITH

(b. 1948–)

B ritish writer Alexander McCall Smith is the creator of the *No. 1 Ladies Detective Agency* series. These novels feature the protagonist Precious Ramotswe, a fictional character who is Botswana's only female detective.

McCall Smith was raised in Southern Rhodesia and moved to Scotland at age 18 to study at the University of Edinburgh. He received a law degree in 1971 and then returned to Africa, where he helped to establish the law school at the University of Botswana. Back at the University of

Edinburgh, where he eventually became a
professor of medical law, he published a range
of scholarly works. He also served as vice-
chairman of the British Human Genetics
Commission. He retired from teaching in
2005 to focus on writing full-time.

*Raised in Rhodesia, author Alexander McCall Smith created
Precious Ramotswe, the Botswanan detective featured
in his* Ladies No. 1 Detective Agency *series.* Raphael
Gaillarde/Gammo-Rapho/Getty Images

In 1976 McCall Smith published his first fiction work, a children's novel. He went on to write more children's books, many of which are set in Africa or derived from African sources. *Children of Wax: African Folk Tales* (1989), a collection aimed at both children and adults, consists of stories he collected in Zimbabwe.

His first novel for adults, *The No. 1 Ladies' Detective Agency*, emerged from a short story McCall Smith had written earlier. First published in Great Britain in 1998, the book was not published in the United States until 2002. By that time McCall Smith had already published two more books centered on Precious Ramotswe. The first book subsequently became an international best seller. By the time the series reached its ninth novel, *The Miracle at Speedy Motors* (2008), more than 15 million copies of the books had been sold in English alone, and *The No. 1 Ladies' Detective Agency* had been adapted as a television series. Throughout the novels, Ramotswe works with her assistant Makutsi and J.L.B. Matekoni to solve mysteries in which crime consists not of murder but of petty burglary, jealousy, and other puzzles of everyday life in Botswana.

McCall Smith is also the author of three other series. *The Sunday Philosophy Club* series, which began with a 2004 novel of the same name, has as its main character Isabel Dalhousie, a philosopher and amateur detective in Edinburgh. The *44 Scotland Street* series began as a serial published in the newspaper the *Scotsman* in 2004 and continued with such books as *The Importance of Being Seven* (2010). Finally, the von Igelfeld series began with *Portuguese Irregular Verbs* (2003), a comic novel about the German academic Dr. Moritz-Maria von Igelfeld.

McCall Smith turned again to serial publication in 2008 with the *Corduroy Mansions* series, which he released in print and as a podcast in weekly installments via the Web site of the British newspaper the *Daily Telegraph*. That year he also published the novel *La's Orchestra Saves the World*, which centers on a newly divorced young woman who founds an amateur orchestra during World War II. McCall Smith himself had conceived such an ensemble in Edinburgh in 1995; it was known as the Really Terrible Orchestra.

McCall Smith also wrote the opera *The Okavango Macbeth*, a reimagining of

William Shakespeare's *Macbeth* set in Botswana with baboons as its main characters. It debuted in 2009 at the No. 1 Ladies' Opera House, a small musical venue that he had opened near Gaborone, Botswana. In 2012 he conceived the idea of a tapestry depicting the history of Scotland; the collaborative project eventually produced more than 150 panels. McCall Smith was made a Commander of the British Empire (CBE) in 2007.

DONALD J. SOBOL

(b. 1924–d. 2012)

American author Donald J. Sobol captivated millions of young readers with his *Encyclopedia Brown* mystery series. The series featured the 10-year-old detective Leroy ("Encyclopedia") Brown, who—aided by his pal Sally Kimball—applies his brilliant observational and deductive skills to crime solving in small-town Idaville, Florida.

Sobol was born on October 4, 1924, in the Bronx, New York. He served in the U.S. Army Corps of Engineers during

World War II and earned a B.A. degree from Oberlin College in Ohio in 1948. He later worked as a newspaper reporter for the *New York Sun* and the *Long Island Daily Press*, and in the late 1950s he started writing "Two-Minute Mysteries," a fiction column. Each of the 29 books in the *Encyclopedia Brown* series—from *Encyclopedia Brown: Boy Detective* (1963) to *Encyclopedia Brown and the Case of the Soccer Scheme* (2012)—consisted of several mystery stories, with the solutions provided only at the end of the book. Sobol believed this would encourage children to solve the cases on their own. The series was adapted for television in 1989.

Sobol wrote more than 80 fiction and nonfiction books altogether. He received an Edgar Award from the Mystery Writers of America in 1976. He died on July 11, 2012, in South Miami, Fla.

MICKEY SPILLANE

(b. 1918–d. 2006)

American writer Mickey Spillane became famous for writing detective fiction characterized by violence and sexual content.

He was born Frank Morrison Spillane on March 9, 1918, in Brooklyn, N.Y. Spillane began his career by writing for pulp magazines and comic books in order to pay for his schooling. His first novel, *I, the Jury* (1947), introduced detective Mike Hammer, who appeared in other works, such as *My Gun Is Quick* (1950) and *The Big Kill* (1951). *Kiss Me, Deadly* (1952) was made into a highly successful movie in 1955.

In the early 1950s Spillane retired from writing after he became a Jehovah's Witness. Ten years later he resumed his career with *The Deep* (1961). He returned to the Mike Hammer series with *The Girl Hunters* (1962). He also wrote the script for and played the role of Hammer in the novel's 1963 film adaptation. Later books in the Hammer series include *The Killing Man* (1989) and *Black Alley* (1996). In addition to movies, the Mike Hammer character was also featured in two popular television series.

Spillane initiated a new book series with *Day of the Guns* (1964), which centered on the international agent Tiger Mann. Among his other books are *The*

Last Cop Out (1973) and the children's book *The Day the Sea Rolled Back* (1979). He died on July 17, 2006, in Murrells Inlet, South Carolina.

R.L. STINE

(b. 1943–)

The American novelist R.L. Stine writes both humor and horror books geared to a young-adult audience. He is best known for two series, the *Goosebumps* and *Fear Street* series.

Robert Lawrence Stine was born on Oct. 8, 1943 in Columbus, Ohio. He graduated from Ohio State University in 1965, having served three years as editor of the campus humor magazine, the *Sundial*. After teaching junior high school for a year, he went to New York City, where he eventually landed an editorial job with Scholastic Books. He worked there for 16 years on various children's magazines, notably *Bananas*, which was written for teens.

The first of Stine's more than 40 humor books for children, *The Absurdly*

Silly Encyclopedia & Fly Swatter (1978), was published under the pseudonym Jovial Bob Stine. His first scary novel, *Blind Date*, was released in 1986 and launched Stine's career as a horror writer. His *Fear Street* series of stories for young teens began with *The New Girl* (1989), and the *Goosebumps* series for 8- to 11-year-olds was launched with *Welcome to Dead House* (1992). The latter series inspired the television program *Goosebumps* (1995–98). The unpredictability, plot twists, and cliff-hanger endings of his horror writing relied on surprise, avoided the seriously threatening topics of modern urban life, and delivered to kids what Stine termed "a safe scare." Both series were an immediate success.

Following this initial success, Stine launched several spin-off series, including *Fear Street Super Chillers* (1991); *Give Yourself Goosebumps* (1995), a choose-your-own-scary-adventure line; and *The Nightmare Room* (2000), which was adapted for television in 2001. In 2008 Stine revived the haunted dummy, a classic *Goosebumps* character, in the first book of the *Goosebumps Horrorland* series, titled

Revenge of the Living Dummy. Other notable series penned by Stine include *Point Horror* (1986) and *Rotten School* (2005).

By 2009 Stine had sold more than 300 million copies of his children's books. He also wrote several novels for adults, including *Superstitious* (1995), *Eye Candy* (2004), and *Red Rain* (2012).

BRAM STOKER

(b. 1847–d. 1912)

The Irish-born writer Bram Stoker is best known as the author of the Gothic horror tale *Dracula*. This immensely popular vampire novel also enjoyed great success in several versions as a play and as a film, including the 1931 classic starring Bela Lugosi.

Abraham (Bram) Stoker was born in Dublin, Ireland, on Nov. 8, 1847. Unable to stand or walk as a child, he was bedridden until he was 7. Eventually he outgrew his weakness to become an outstanding athlete at the University of Dublin. He worked for 10 years in the civil service at

The most infamous vampire of them all, Count Dracula,
was the creation of Irish-born writer Bram Stoker.
Hulton Archive/Getty Images

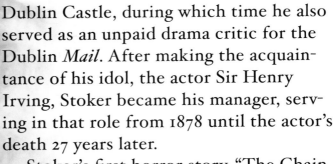

Dublin Castle, during which time he also served as an unpaid drama critic for the Dublin *Mail*. After making the acquaintance of his idol, the actor Sir Henry Irving, Stoker became his manager, serving in that role from 1878 until the actor's death 27 years later.

Stoker's first horror story, "The Chain of Destiny," was published in 1875. *The Snake's Pass*, his first novel, was published in 1890, and in 1897 his masterpiece, *Dracula*, appeared. The latter tells the story of Count Dracula, a vampire from Transylvania who makes his way to England and there victimizes innocent people to gain the blood on which he lives. It is written chiefly in the form of journals and letters written by the principal characters—Jonathan Harker, who makes the first contact with Dracula; Mina, Jonathan's wife; Dr. Seward; and Lucy Westenra, a victim who herself becomes a vampire. Led by Dr. Van Helsing, Harker and his friends eventually overpower and destroy Dracula.

Stoker wrote several other novels— among them *The Mystery of the Sea* (1902), *The Jewel of Seven Stars* (1904), and *The Lady*

of the Shroud (1909)—but none of them approached the popularity, or, indeed, the quality, of *Dracula*. He died in London on April 20, 1912.

REX STOUT

(b. 1886–d. 1975)

American author Rex Stout was the creator of the eccentric and reclusive detective Nero Wolfe. Stout's mystery stories revolve around the escapades of Wolfe and his wisecracking aide, Archie Goodwin.

Stout was born on Dec. 1, 1886, in Nobelsville, Ind. He worked odd jobs until 1912, when he began to write sporadically for magazines. After writing four moderately successful novels, Stout turned to the form of the detective story. In *Fer-de-Lance* (1934) he introduced Nero Wolfe, the obese, brilliant aesthete who solves crimes without leaving his New York City brownstone house. Wolfe has, as did Stout, a passion for gourmet foods and gardening. The mysteries are narrated by Archie Goodwin, Wolfe's link to the outside world.

Stout wrote 46 Wolfe mysteries; the well-written books have remained very popular. Stout was active in numerous organizations supporting democracy and world federalism, including the Writers Board for World Government. He died in Danbury, Conn., on Oct. 27, 1975.

EDWARD STRATEMEYER

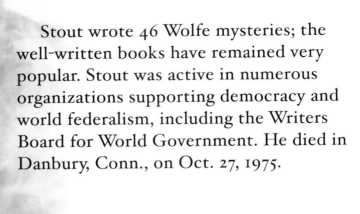

(b. 1862–d. 1930)

Edward Stratemeyer was an american writer of popular juvenile fiction, and his Stratemeyer Literary Syndicate (1906–84) produced such books as the *Rover Boys* series, the *Hardy Boys* series, the *Tom Swift* series, the *Bobbsey Twins* series, and the *Nancy Drew* series.

Stratemeyer was born in Elizabeth, N.J., on Oct. 4, 1862. He worked as a store clerk and, on the side, began writing stories in imitation of those of Horatio Alger and popular adventure writers, selling his first magazine story in 1888. In the following decade he became editor of

Good News (1893–95), for which he wrote boys' stories, and of his own journal, *Bright Days* (1896). His first book, *Richard Dare's Venture*, appeared in 1894, the first in a series, and about 1896 he began writing concurrently several series, such as the *Rover Boys' Series for Young Americans*, beginning in 1899, and the *Boy Hunters* series, beginning in 1906. Over the years he wrote hundreds of books and stories.

In 1906 Stratemeyer founded the Stratemeyer Literary Syndicate, which published various juvenile series, written by himself and others. (Any one series might have had several authors, all using the same pseudonym.) The *Hardy Boys* books, the first of which was published in 1927, feature fictional teen detective brothers Frank and Joe Hardy. More than four dozen novels about the Hardys were written by "Franklin W. Dixon"—the pseudonym used by a series of writers, including Stratemeyer—continuously from 1927. A *Hardy Boys Casefiles* series was published in 1987–98 and averaged about 10 titles a year. Carolyn Keene was the pseudonym for the author of more than 100 *Nancy Drew* novels published from 1930 through 1990. The character Nancy

Drew has been featured in a number of films, including a 2007 theatrical release starring Emma Roberts.

After Stratemeyer's death on May 10, 1930, his company was largely directed by his daughter, Harriet Stratemeyer Adams (1892–1982). Under pseudonyms she and writers such as Mildred Wirt Benson and Leslie McFarlane wrote many of the novels in the *Nancy Drew, Dana Girls, Hardy Boys,* and *Bobbsey Twins* series. In 1984 the publisher Simon & Schuster acquired all rights to the Stratemeyer Literary Syndicate.

PETER STRAUB

(b. 1943–)

Originally a poet, Peter Straub turned to writing horror novels.

Peter Francis Straub was born in Milwaukee, Wisc., on March 2, 1943. The eldest of three sons, he spent a great deal of his childhood reading and concocting stories. Straub attended the Milwaukee Country Day School on scholarship, and went on to the University of Wisconsin, earning a bachelor's degree in 1963, followed by a master's degree in literature from Columbia University in 1966. He returned to his alma mater, Country Day, to teach English.

After three years at Country Day, Straub moved to Dublin, Ire., in pursuit of his Ph.D. There he spent the years from 1969 to 1972 writing and studying poetry, eventually publishing two volumes of his verse. With the publication of his first novel, *Marriages* (1972), Straub abandoned academia and became a full-time novelist, spending the next seven years in London before returning to America.

His early novels, *Julia* (1975; film, 1981, released as *The Haunting of Julia*) and *If You Could See Me Now* (1976) show the emergence of a theme in his works: the concept that digging into one's past misdeeds affects the present, and that guilt plays with one's mind. His characters are neither wholly good nor evil, but a very human mix of the two.

Subsequent works by Straub include *Ghost Story* (1979; film, 1981), *Shadowlands* (1980), *Koko* (1988), *Mr. X* (1999), *A Dark Matter* (2010), and *Mrs. God* (2012). He collaborated with horror-novelist Stephen

King on 1984's *The Talisman* and its sequel, *Black House* (2010).

Straub has received numerous awards in his main genre of horror, most recently the Bram Stoker Award for the collection *5 Stories* (2007). In addition to writing, Straub also has edited the anthology *Poe's Children: The New Horror.*

MARGARET SUTTON

(b. 1903–d. 2001)

Margaret Sutton is best known for her *Judy Bolton* mystery stories. The young detective Bolton was a feminist role model for her time.

Sutton was born Rachel Beebe on Jan. 22, 1903 in Odin, Pennsylvania. She graduated from the Rochester Business Institute in Rochester, N.Y. in 1920, and worked as a secretary and in the printing business for several years. She married in 1924, moved to Long Island, N.Y. and had five children. It was through writing stories for her daughter that she honed her talent, thus on her way toward a career as a novelist.

The first *Judy Bolton* novel, *The Vanishing Shadow* (1932), was based on a real-life event: the failure of the Austin Dam in 1911. Subsequent books would also borrow happenings and places from Sutton's life and the world at large.

Unlike many other children's book characters, Judy Bolton grew up, got married and became guardian to a young girl over the course of the series, which ended after 38 novels in 1967. A 39th, *The Strange Likeness*, was planned but never published. Some speculated that the series was cancelled to take away competition from the *Nancy Drew* books, but it is more likely that interest was waning in the long-running series.

Sutton published other books, including a series about a nurse named Gail Gardner and some children's historical fiction. She taught creative writing to adults, was a public speaker, and involved in social causes, such as civil rights and fair housing.

Sutton died on June 21, 2001, in Lock Haven, Pa. In 2012, a Judy Bolton Weekend

was held in Coudersport, Penn. It included tours of the locations that were featured in the series.

SCOTT TUROW

(b. 1949–)

S cott Turow is a lawyer turned best-selling suspense novelist. He is the creator of a genre of crime and suspense novels dealing with law and the legal profession.

Turow was born on April 12, 1949, in Chicago, Ill. He received a Juris Doctor (J.D.) degree in 1978 from Harvard University. While there he published a nonfiction work, *One L: What They Really Teach You at Harvard Law School* (1977), that is considered classic reading for law students.

Turow's first novel, *Presumed Innocent* (1987; film, 1990), was written while he was working as an assistant U.S. attorney in Chicago (1978–86). The story follows Rusty Sabich, a deputy prosecutor who is assigned to investigate the murder of a female colleague with whom he had had an affair. *The Burden of Proof* (1990; television film, 1992)

and *Pleading Guilty* (1993; television film, 2010) continue in the vein of legal drama, although the former focuses more on troubles at home faced by its protagonist.

Turow's later works include *The Laws of Our Fathers* (1996) and *Personal Injuries* (1999). In *Ordinary Heroes* (2005) a crime reporter discovers papers that reveal the truth about his father's court-martial during World War II. *Innocent* (2010; television film, 2011) is a sequel to *Presumed Innocent.* Turow also edited the two-volume *Guilty as Charged: A Mystery Writers of America Anthology* (1996, 1997). His nonfiction book *Ultimate Punishment: A Lawyer's Reflections on Dealing with the Death Penalty* was published in 2003.

In addition to pursuing his writing career, Turow continued to practice law. In 1986 he joined a private firm, where he focused on white-collar crimes and pro bono work.

EDGAR WALLACE

(b. 1875–d. 1932)

The British novelist, playwright, and journalist Edgar Wallace produced

Suspense writer Edgar Wallace, posing for photographers at his desk in the 1930s. Sasha/Hulton Archive/Getty Images

enormously popular detective and suspense stories. Some critic believe he practically invented the modern thriller.

Richard Horatio Edgar Wallace was born in London, England, on April 1, 1875. He left school at the age of 12 and held a variety of odd jobs until he joined the army at 18; he served in South Africa until 1899, when he became a reporter. He returned to England and produced his first success, a story of vigilante justice entitled *The Four Just Men* (1905), which he sold outright for a small amount.

Wallace's works in the mystery and suspense genre have complex but clearly developed plots and are known for their exciting climaxes. His literary output—175 books, 15 plays, and countless articles and review sketches—was enormous, and his rate of production so great as to be the subject of humor. His books include *Private Shelby* (1909), *Sanders of the River* (1911), *The Crimson Circle* (1922), *The Green Archer* (1923), *The Flying Squad* (1928), *The Terror* (1930), and *On the Spot* (1931). His last work was part-authorship of the film script for *King Kong* (1933).

Wallace died in Hollywood, Calif., on February 10, 1932. His literary reputation has

suffered since his death, partly because of the conservative values espoused in his works.

DONALD E. WESTLAKE

(b. 1933–d. 2008)

Author Donald E. Westlake attracted a wide readership as well as great critical acclaim with his stylish crime novels. Westlake published more than 100 novels during his lifetime.

Donald Edwin Westlake was born July 12, 1933, in Brooklyn, N.Y. He expressed an interest in becoming a writer at an early age, pecking out stories about gangsters, cowboys, and aliens on a manual type-writer beginning at age eleven. Westlake attended three colleges in New York State, but graduated from none of them. (The last he attended, which is now the State University of New York at Binghamton gave him an honorary doctorate in 1996.)

Westlake's first published novel, *The Mercenaries* (1960; also published as *The*

Smashers and *The Cutie*) features a gang-ster turned detective looking for the woman who set up a colleague to take a murder rap. One of the author's best-known characters was the hapless thief John Dortmunder, the protagonist of such novels as *The Hot Rock* (1970), *Bank Shot* (1972), *Why Me?* (1983), and *What's So Funny?* (2007). Writing as Richard Stark—one of numerous pseudonyms Westlake employed during his career—he also cre-ated a popular series of novels featuring another thief, a ruthless criminal known simply as Parker. Among the many titles in the Parker series are *The Hunter* (1962), *The Outfit* (1963), *The Score* (1964), and *Slayground* (1971).

Westlake earned an Academy Award nomination in 1991 for his screenplay for the film *The Grifters* (1990). He won the Mystery Writers of America's Edgar Allan Poe Award three times, and the organi-zation bestowed on him the title Grand Master—its highest honor—in 1993. Westlake died on vacation in San Tancho, Mexico, on Dec. 31, 2008. He was on his way to a New Year's Eve dinner when he suffered a heart attack.

L.R. WRIGHT

(b. 1939–d. 2001)

Canadian novelist L.R. Wright was internationally known for her crime novels. Many of her works featured detective Karl Alberg of the Royal Canadian Mounted Police, her most popular character.

Laurali Rose Appleby, known as "Bunny," was born on June 5, 1939, in Saskatoon, Saskatchewan, Canada. She married John Wright, whom she met while performing in children's theater, in 1962. For a time L.R. Wright was a reporter and editor for newspapers in Calgary, Alberta, Canada. After taking a writing course, she quit and dedicated herself to writing fiction full time.

Wright's first novel, *Neighbours* (1979), won the Alberta Best First Novel Award. The first of her *Karl Alberg* series, *The Suspect* (1985), won the Mystery Writers of America's Edgar Allen Poe Award for best crime novel. Two later Alberg mysteries, *A Chill Rain in January* (1990) and *Mother Love* (1995), received the Crime Writers of Canada's Arthur Ellis Award.

Wright died of cancer on Feb. 25, 2001, in Vancouver. Her novel *Menace* (2001) was published posthumously.

Glossary

aesthete One who is, or yearns to be, sensitive to all things beautiful, especially within the arts.

anthology A collection of selected literary pieces or passages or works of art or music.

cynical Distrustful of others, particularly on the assumption that their motives are selfish.

dysgraphia Marked by the inability to write neatly and coherently.

feminist One who believes in, and fights for, gender equality and the rights of women.

feudalism A political or social system in which homage is paid to the one in power.

Gothic A style of fiction characterized by the use of remote settings and mysterious or violent occurrences.

idyllic Something that is pleasant due to its simplicity.

novella A story that is longer than a traditional short story but not quite as long or involved as a novel.

ominous Foreboding or foretelling of evil.

pro bono Refers to professional work, particularly legal work, done for free and for the public good.

prolific Marked by being especially productive and inventive.

protagonist The principal character in a work of literature.

serial Something that appears in successive parts or numbers.

sleuth Another term for a detective, or one who investigates the true character of a person or event.

suspense Marked by uncertainty about the eventual outcome.

For More Information

Crime Writers of Canada (CWC)
2160 Colonel William Parkway
Oakville, ON
L6M 0B8
Canada
(905) 582-0967
Web site: http://www.crimewriterscanada.com
Founded in 1982, the CWC is a nonprofit
organization for writers, readers, and lovers
of Canadian crime writing. It sponsors the
Arthur Ellis Awards for Crime and Mystery
Writing in recognition of esteemed
crime and mystery writers, and provides
resources for writers and fans of crime
writing on the latest developments in the
genre.

Edgar Allan Poe Society of Baltimore
1610 Dogwood Hill Road
Towson, MD 21286
(410) 821-1285
Web site: http://www.eapoe.org
The Edgar Allan Poe Society of Baltimore
is a nonprofit organization that publishes and promotes information on
Poe's life and works, and works to pre-
serve sites of historical importance
to his legacy. The group sponsors an
annual lecture and commemorative

gathering roughly on the anniversary of his death.

Friends of Mystery
P.O. Box 8251
Portland, OR 97207
(503) 244-5271
Web site: http://www.friendsofmystery.org
Friends of Mystery is a nonprofit literary organization dedicated to the promotion of educational study of the mystery genre. It sponsors weekly public meetings and a reading group, and publishes a bimonthly newsletter called the *Blood-Letter.* It also offers the annual Spotted Owl Award for the best mystery work by a Pacific Northwest author.

Horror Writers Association (HWA)
244 5th Avenue, Suite 2767
New York, NY 10001
Web site: http://www.horror.org
The HWA is one of the largest international organizations promoting public interest in horror and dark fantasy literature. It coordinates public readings, lectures, book signings by horror writers, and maintains a presence at major horror and fantasy conventions. It also

publishes a newsletter and bestows the annual Bram Stoker Awards for excellence in horror literature.

International Association of Crime Writers (IACW), North American Branch
328 8th Avenue, #114
New York, NY 10001
(212) 753-3915
Web site: http://www.crimewritersna.org
The IACW is an international organization that promotes crime and mystery writing around the world, particularly the translation and promotion of works across national borders. The North American branch publishes the *Border Patrol* quarterly newsletter, sponsors social events for fans and writers, and compiles anthologies of crime writing.

Mystery Readers International (MRI)
Box 8116
Berkeley, CA 94707
Web site: http://www.mysteryreaders.org
MRI is one of the largest mystery fan organizations in the world, with membership spanning all fifty states and eighteen countries abroad. It publishes the *Mystery Readers Journal*, promotes reading groups,

and holds member votes annually to award the Macavity Awards for various categories in the mystery genre.

Mystery Writers of America (MWA)
1140 Broadway, Suite 1507
New York NY 10001
(212) 888-8171
Web site: http://www.mysterywriters.org
Since 1945, the MWA has been a top organization in the field of mystery and crime writers, professionals, and fans. It hosts the Edgar Awards each spring and coordinates symposiums and events for mystery and crime authors and readers. Each of the eleven regional chapters publishes a newsletter and has regular meetings, open to members and nonmembers alike.

Web Sites

Due to the changing nature of Internet links, Rosen Educational Services has developed an online list of Web sites related to the subject of this book. This site is updated regularly. Please use this link to access the list:

http://www.rosenlinks.com/eafct/myst

For Further Reading

Golla, Robert. *Conversations with Michael Crichton.* Jackson, MS: University Press of Mississippi, 2011.

Hamilton, Sue. *Masters of Horror.* Edina, MN: ABDO Publishing, 2007.

Hopkins, Lisa. *Bram Stoker: A Literary Life.* New York, NY: Palgrave MacMillan, 2007.

King, Stephen. *On Writing.* New York, NY: Scribner, 2010.

Nevins, Francis M. *The Anthony Boucher Chronicles: Review and Commentary 1942-1947.* Vancleave, MS: Ramble House, 2009.

Schoell, William. *H.P. Lovecraft: Master of Weird Fiction.* Greensboro, NC: Morgan Reynolds, 2004.

Sheen, Barbara. *Stephanie Meyer: Twilight Saga Author.* San Diego: Kidhaven, 2010.

Stine, R.L. *It Came From Ohio: My Life as a Writer.* New York, NY: Scholastic, Inc., 1998.

Streissguth, Tom. *Edgar Allan Poe.* Minneapolis, MN: Lerner, 2007.

Wells, Catherine. *Strange Creatures: The Story of Mary Shelley.* Greensboro, NC: Morgan Reynolds, 2009.

Index